Best Wishes.

Helen's Journey

The Story of One Couple's Faith and Love in a Battle with Cancer

H. David Goldsmith

Xulon
PRESS

Copyright © 2011 by H. David Goldsmith

Helen's Journey
The story of one couple's faith and love in a battle with cancer
by H. David Goldsmith

Printed in the United States of America

ISBN 9781619043336

All rights reserved solely by the author. The author guarantees all contents are original and do not infringe upon the legal rights of any other person or work. No part of this book may be reproduced in any form without the permission of the author. The views expressed in this book are not necessarily those of the publisher.

Unless otherwise indicated, Bible quotations are taken from The King James Bible.

www.xulonpress.com

Dedicated to my children

Amy

Steve and Kristen

Peter and Jocelyn

Mike and Lian

Who loved their mother dearly and miss her greatly.

Who stood shoulder to shoulder with Helen and I

during her illness, and at the time of her passing,

like a Roman shield wall, encompassing, protecting,

and caring for us both

Introduction

On July 28, 2008, my loving wife Helen was diagnosed with breast cancer. On October 16, 2010, she slipped into the presence of our Lord, with only about 20 seconds of concern, sitting on her own bed, in her own bedroom, in her own house, peacefully, gently, painlessly, with my arm around her. God writes really good scripts.

Between those two dates Helen fought cancer with every fiber in her being as I supported her to the best of my ability. In September of 2008, she started a blog, *The purpose of* [which] *is to keep friends and loved ones up to date on the events of my cancer journey. I appreciate so much that so many people are caring about me and praying for me at this time.*

At the same time I started a journal, talking about the cares and concerns of fighting cancer, the low days, and the happy days. We had long talks about our love for God and for each other, and talked about the nature of both of our funeral services, picking out music, scripture, and determining who would be involved. We organized our affairs, updating wills, powers of attorney, beneficiaries on life insurance policies, purchased our burial plots, pre-planned and started pre-paying our funerals. It may sound like a difficult topic of conversation, but we planned everything for <u>both</u> of us with the goal of making things simple for our children when my time comes, and to avoid the image of rushing to get things ready for Helen's death.

When Helen's "graduation" came, we had all temporal arrangements made, and there was no need to react in a panic as so many families do upon the sudden death of a loved one, scrambling to plan a funeral. I was still not prepared for the suddenness of her death, especially when it appeared that her health was improving. I do not believe anyone can be prepared for a loved one to take that last breath. One of our children had left Toronto on a business trip to Tel Aviv, and was airborne for three hours after his mother's death before we could reach him. The earliest return flight he could get was Wednesday (Helen died on a Saturday evening) and so we planned the funeral for a full week after Helen's death, to give family members time to travel from British Columbia, Minnesota, Texas, Washington State, Florida, and across Ontario and Quebec. This gave us time to assemble, to grieve, to reminisce, to thoughtfully prepare the obituary notice, the order of service, and to confirm funeral arrangements with our church pastor and the funeral home. As I reflect back, I question why we seem to be in such a hurry to get bodies into the ground. Other than religious customs, I don't know why we are in such a rush. The extra time let us as a family relax, and enjoy the funeral. After all this was Helen's graduation to Glory.

About six weeks before her death, Helen and I were talking one evening about funeral services. Suddenly she began to laugh in the rich contralto voice that I loved to hear. I asked "what's so funny?" She replied, "I just thought of what processional music I want when my casket is rolled into the church for my funeral." "That's funny?" I asked. With her face beaming and her huge smile, she said "This is going to be my graduation, and by golly I want graduation music. I want to come in to the strains of 'Pomp and Circumstance." So, I went on-line and found an orchestral version of "Pomp and Circumstance," and to that stirring music, we as a family walked with our heads held high behind

Helen's casket, celebrating her life and the way she had touched so many people.

Many people after the funeral sent me notes or called me to tell me what an "uplifting event" her funeral service was. When one knows beyond a shadow of a doubt that for a child of Christ "to be absent from the body is to be present with the Lord," death does not represent an end, but rather a beginning of a life eternal and a promise of a wonderful reunion in the future.

With this book I hope to share with you, the readers, a glimpse into how a fervent faith and a binding love can help travel this road. I will share with you scriptures that were supportive to us, a prayer of faith that Helen wrote during her journey, and some observations and suggestions that may be beneficial to you.

I want to be open with all of you right from the outset, that I was by no means a perfect husband. In the early years of our marriage I was verbally abusive and overbearing. One morning Helen sat on the edge of the bed with the most profound look of sadness on her face. When I asked what her problem was, she replied "I am not sure that I want to go on being married to you." That was a wakeup call for me. Our children were all of an age that we were able to put all four in a summer camp, and Helen and I made our way to Owen Sound Ontario, where we spent a week talking, and praying and crying and loving as we discussed the wrinkles in our marriage (mostly mine) and what we needed to do to correct them. I made a vow to Helen that I would be a different husband, and with God's help, in the years since, I believe I have kept that vow.

Throughout the book, I will place extracts from Helen's blog in *italics* so you can distinguish her own words from mine. I will also include some (not all) comments posted on Helen's blog by family, friends and especially current and former students, whose lives Helen touched through this journey.

Chapter One

Coming Together

This story starts in September of 1963, in the chapel of London College of Bible and Missions, in London, Ontario. The school had a 48 voice a capella choir, and auditions were underway for the 1963-64 choir. A piece of music had been distributed, and the hopeful candidates were arrayed with sopranos in front of the tenors and altos in front of the basses. In the back row of the altos was a young lady from Ottawa, Ontario, who had been president of her high school choir in her senior year and a soloist for several years, and in the front row of the basses was a young man from Chatham, Ontario, who had spent four years at Prairie Bible Institute in Three Hills, Alberta and had already had one year of voice lessons there.

The director's hand came down on the downbeat and 48 voices burst into song. The young Ottawa lady whipped her head around to see where "that voice" was coming from, and the young Chatham man looked at her and thought: that is the most beautiful girl I have ever seen!

Ottawa gal had arrived in London on the train on crutches because of foot surgery almost immediately prior to travel. She probably should have arrived a week or two later, but was determined not to miss one minute of the school year. One of the orientation events in the first two week included a sunrise breakfast in Fanshaw Park near London, the parking lot of which was surrounded by thick wooden posts through which a chain was strung. As Ottawa gal leaned on her crutches contemplating how to traverse this barrier, Chatham guy saw a chance, and calling to one of his friends, ran over and picked up Ottawa gal, and passed her over the chain to his friend. Obviously, this necessitated Chatham guy to stay very close to Ottawa gal for the duration of the breakfast, should there be any other insurmountable obstacles, which he could assist Ottawa gal to transverse thus showing how chivalrous he was.

Things were somewhat complicated by the fact that Chatham guy was dating a young woman in Toronto, but over time, Ottawa gal and Chatham guy got to know each other sitting together in classes, sharing tables in the cafeteria, and going out as part of large groups for pizza, and to take part in "hootenannies" in local coffee shops. By about Christmas of 1965, Chatham guy and Ottawa gal had begun to think that it was more fun to go out without the large group and on February 14th, 1965, Valentine's Day, the first "official date" took place. Chatham guy was a smart cookie, and it only took until August of 1965 for him to take Ottawa gal "off the market," by getting down on one knee and asking for her hand in marriage. This provided quite a shock to Ottawa gal's parents who finally agreed on the condition that no wedding was to take place until the LCBM degree was safely in Ottawa gal's hand in 1967. This proposal took place at a Monument on Highway 2 just east of Thamesville, Ontario, dedicated to the Pawnee Indian Chief Tecumseh, who with his people, fought along side of the British in the war between Britain and the United States from 1812 to 1814, and who died on that spot. For years later every time the family drove by that monument, a sonorous voice from one of the boys in the back seat of the car would say "A lot of great men have fallen there."

While still in college together, Chatham guy wanted to give Ottawa gal flowers, but could not afford to splurge, so he began to give Ottawa gal on occasion, corsages made of a single red rose, which she would wear to class. Little did Chatham guy know that he had begun a tradition that would carry on for 45 years.

Fast forward to June 17th of 1967, and Helen Miller and David Goldsmith made a pledge in front of God and witnesses, in Calvary Baptist Church in Ottawa that they would love and honour each other and care for each other in times of health & sickness, good times & bad times, flush times & and financially strapped times, for the rest of their lives. They have done that and now, just over 43 years later, Helen has been chosen to be the first of the duo to enter into Glory.

In the fall of 1967 Helen attended the Windsor Teacher's College on the advice of her father who said she needed the ability to support herself if anything happened to me. She graduated on the Dean's honour list, and in September 1968 began teaching at Queen Mary School in

Chatham. In May of 1973, Amy Catharine came to grace our home and complicate our lives, and Helen started a two year leave of absence from teaching. What might have transpired at the end of the two years was never to be known, because in the spring of 1974 we discovered Stephen David was on the way, and any thoughts of going back to teaching at the end of the two years dissipated, when Steve was born in September of 1974.

In March of 1977 Peter James joined us, and in March of 1979 Michael Andrew arrived to make our family complete.

Helen absolutely revered her children. It would be 18 years before she would return to full-time teaching. We were fortunate that I had a good salary, and together we were willing to make sacrifices that would enable us to buy swing sets, and make sand-boxes and jungle gyms, while taking on what seemed like huge mortgage payments. Between the birth of Stephen and Peter we were able to build and move into a new home with over an acre of land, with a huge back yard in which to play, a home we have shared together for more than 35 years, and one with so many delightful memories.

Our children were either fortunate or unfortunate to be born to an elementary school teacher. Their early lives were filled with stories, books, music, Sesame Street and the Polka Dot Door TV programs, trips to museums and libraries, picnics along the St. Clair River in Port Lambton and days at the beach in Erieau, on the shore of Lake Erie. Each one was reading very well on the first day of kindergarten, and each provided a special challenge for teachers because of their advanced capabilities. Helen was right along side of each of them as their educational journeys unfolded. She knew what resources were available in schools, and frankly what was missing from the educational system. At a time when the Ministry of Education decided to introduce something called "whole language" to the classrooms, which was a form of educated guessing at what a word might be by its context, Helen made display charts on large pieces of Bristol board, teaching her children phonics at home. Like the proverbial "mama grizzly" she wanted what was best for her children, and was prepared to stop at nothing to achieve it. Her drive to ensure the best possible education for our children continued right through their university careers.

As the children matured, and began to be involved in sports, both in school and in public leagues, no one was a more vocal fan than Helen. One son in minor hockey complained at one point "Mom you are so loud I can hear you all over the arena, even with my helmet on." I guess it was those four years of voice lessons. Another son made the claim that Mom was so loud that she even drowned out the lady with the cow bell. Actually there were three very vociferous fans supporting minor hockey those days, and by unspoken agreement with the other parents, Helen, the lady with the cow bell and a gentle, bearded man nicknamed "The Bear" all sat huddled together in the farthest corner of Ericson arena with wide open spaces between them and the rest of the fans.

One of her greatest contributions to her children Helen made through prayer. She prayed daily for all of her children. Even when they were pre-teens, she prayed for the life partners they would choose, for the careers they would pursue, and most of all for them to come to their own personal relationship with God. She prayed for her children right up to the last day of her life.

Helen was a woman of tenacious faith, a loving partner, a dedicated mother, a wonderful musician, and a committed and outgoing teacher. She touched lives through her personality, her music, her "grand piano smile," her infectious laugh, and her genuine interest in the well being of other people. She treasured her children, including our "chosen daughters," chosen for us by our sons. She reveled in her grandchildren, delighted to see them growing and maturing, whether in person or through frequent "Skype" sessions.

She was a soul mate, companion, lover, and friend to me for over 45 years, 43 of those as my bride. I was incredibly proud of her and her accomplishments. She was more than my "better half," she was my strength, my joy, my "pull me back down to earth dose of realism" person, my comfort in sickness, pain and times of sadness, but also my high-kickin' partner in times of great joy. I will miss her deeply. It was my privilege to be her husband and friend for more than 43 years!

In that 1964 choir that I spoke of above we sang a song entitled *When He Shall Come.* In between two of the verses, as the choir hummed, a gentleman from Zambia, named

Kosamo Kosanso, with a marvelous deep voice like James Earl Jones would quote a reading "What are these which are arrayed in white robes, and whence came they? These are they which came out of great tribulation, and have washed their robes and made them white in the blood of the Lamb."

As I looked at Helen on her bed just as she had fallen back and before I could react, I had an image pop into my mind of her in her white robe, slipping into the alto section of the magnificent choir of Heaven, turning to the person next to her and saying "what page are we on?"

My relationship with Helen is not ended. It has just been paused. I have the confidence and assurance in God's word, that there will come a day that I will join her, and if I pass the audition, will sing with her again in that great choir praising our Lord and Saviour.

Helen was a very special person. She got to touch the future. She taught !

One of our sons works in the aerospace industry and Helen was astonished at the size of the wings and other parts that Pete was able to help create for airplanes like the big double-decker Airbus A380, or the new Boeing 787. She looked forward to a trip on one of these planes and envisioned being able to look around as she boarded, and say to herself "My son helped make this." (We often joked that after having said this, we would turn around and run like crazy right off the plane.) This, however, was not to be and instead on the evening of October, 16th, 2010 she took a trip in a fashion that Airbus or Boeing can only dream about.

Chapter Two

The Diagnosis

In December of 2000, I along with 171 of my colleagues was furloughed by my employer in Ohio. I was only 55, but I was exhausted from the pressures of work and travel, much of it international travel, for 34 years, and I took this as an opportunity to retire.

On March 30th of 2002, our son Steve married a delightful West Texas gal from Odessa, with the surname of Patton and backbone of titanium! Kristen and Steve met at the same company in Austin, and had dated for almost four years. During that time Helen and I had truly fallen in love with this young woman, and we were incredibly happy to have her become our first "chosen daughter."

In January of 2005 Clayton David Goldsmith joined the Austin household, a first grandchild for Helen and I. In the first year of Clay's life, Helen and I made six trips to Austin. Helen luxuriated in the role of Grandmother. Shortly after his first birthday, Clay was attempting to say Grandma and Grandpa. What came out of his mouth was something like "Bukka" which thrilled Helen. So Bukka she became to Clay and subsequently his two sisters. I am an elected public school board trustee, and over the past eight years this has given me the opportunity to be exposed to and learn about Canada's First Nations. I suggested to our son that he see if Clay could say "Mishoo" which is from the Ojibway name for Grandfather. It clicked and I am proudly known as Mishoo to not only my grandchildren, but all of their cousins.

Helen loved teaching. To her it was a profession, not a job, and she struggled for two years about retiring. On the one hand trips to Texas were very appealing, but on the other hand she could not bring herself to envision a day when she was not in the classroom

Finally in January of 2007 she made her decision, wrote her letter of resignation to the school board, and retired at the end of June 2007. At the time of her retirement, Helen had been teaching French as a second language, a mandatory course in Ontario from grade 1 through grade 10. For the fall semester, a young lady was hired, fluent in French, to take over the teaching of this language to grades 5 through 8 at the elementary school where Helen had taught.

On the first school day in September, Helen went to a boisterous breakfast for retired teachers, aptly named "To Hell with the Bell" and enjoyed every minute of it. In September we made a few day trips to one place and another, and then in October booked a train trip to Quebec City.. When we arrived in Quebec City we were numb in places after 16 hours of travel, but joyful to have run away, and wallowed in the freedom we had to do nothing, or anything we wanted. We spent 10 lovely days in a *pension* in Quebec City, strolling through the Old Town, enjoying the fresh air and the food and wine, making maximum use of the command of the French language that we both had, and participating in the *joie de vive* that only the French can express. At the end of the 10 days, we returned to Chatham, began to plan Christmas and more future trips in the new year.

Schools in Ontario take a Spring break for the third week in March. In February, Helen learned that the young woman who had replaced her had tendered her resignation and was leaving the school and the city as of the March break. Our retirement program with the Board of Education allowed retired teachers to return to the classroom for a maximum of 90 days in each of the three years following retirement. The school principal contacted Helen in a dilemma. The teaching role was a rotary position, whereby the French teacher moved from class to class throughout the school day, and taught the language to classes in grades 5 through 8. Helen had already been involved with the students in the grade 6 to 8 classes in her final year, and already knew which students loved the language and were eager to learn, and those students who were a bit more reluctant. The principal had the option of hiring a teacher for the job from within the school board system on a permanent basis, but because of language in the contract between the school board and the teachers' federation, this would involve "bumping" and as many as six teaching positions might be affected across the system, not even limited to one school. The alternative was to hire a temporary teacher for the remaining three months of the school year and then fill the position permanently for the resumption of classes in September. Helen, who was missing her students greatly, jumped at the chance to go back into the classrooms for three months.

From about 1995, when she turned 50, Helen had been in a screening program for a mammogram every two years. About 2002 she received a telephone call one day from the coordinator of this program telling her that it was time for her biannual scan. Helen commented that it had only been a year since her last check, and the woman replied that there was something wrong with their system, that it was too early for Helen to come in, and that they would contact her the next year. For some unknown reason, at that point Helen seemed to fall off the screening radar, and the call never came in 2003, or any year thereafter. In March of 2002 we were all in Texas for Steve and Kristen's wedding, in

April of 2002 my condo in Ohio finally sold, and I moved back to Canada. In the excitement and bustle of that time and the months that followed, we both seemed to forget about mammograms and none were scheduled.

With her return to teaching in the Spring of 2008, Helen began to experience significant fatigue and loss of energy. She attributed this to being out of shape since her retirement, and the weight of the cart on which she had all of the French textbooks and teaching materials, which had to be moved from classroom to classroom during the day.

In April of 2008, she felt a lump in one breast. She asked me to feel it, and it felt about the size of a grape. Many years ago she had found another lump in her breast, which drove us into panic, but which turned out to be a benign cyst, that was removed in a doctor's office. For two reasons in 2008 Helen did nothing about seeking medical attention for this new lump.

First she assumed it was just another cyst. Secondly, she could not bring herself to disrupt the learning experience for her students, and determined to stick it out until the end of the school year, at the end of June.

In the late Spring of 2008 a good friend in Dallas lost his wife to a seven year battle with cancer. On July 4th of 2008, a dear friend in Dublin Ohio lost his wife to cancer after a multi-year fight, during which time she had gone into remission, had all of her hair grow back in, was loving life, and taking a course to become a real estate agent. When we went to her memorial service in Dublin on July 7th, our minds were now very focused on "the C word."

Back in Chatham after Marilyn's memorial service, Helen and I went to our family doctor. He sent her for a mammogram. It showed the lump, which by now was about the size of a walnut. This was followed by a needle biopsy of the tissue, and on July 28th, we returned together to the doctor's office to be told Helen had breast cancer.

Chapter Three

The Surgery

Obviously this was a shock to both of us, and many tears flowed; mine, Helen's and the nurse who was attempting to comfort us. At that point the Canadian medical system kicked into high gear. Unlike some countries where the family doctor would have remained closely attached to the process, we were immediately put in the hands of specialists. The first contact was a skillful surgeon who specialized in breast removals. Helen, fearing the appearance of a missing breast asked if there was any chance of having only a lumpectomy. The surgeon said that was a possibility, but laid out all of the facts for us. He said that many patients of his had requested lumpectomies, only to be very upset at the disfigured portion of the breast that remained and most returned asking for a full mastectomy. He also talked about the size of the tumour based on the mammogram and some ultrasound images. He said that it was quite large, growing very rapidly, and that he was concerned that he might not get enough clearance between the tumour and Helen's chest wall. His goal was to have 1 cm of clear space between the tumour and surrounding tissue. In actual fact when he did the surgery, he was only able to get 1 mm of clear space.

From the surgeon we were handed to the care of an oncologist in Windsor. The province of Ontario has chosen to aggregate health care skills at centres of excellence in major cities across the province. While surgery and some treatment was available to us in Chatham, the best and the brightest of the specialists were either in London, 70 miles to our East, or Windsor, 50 miles to our West.

At this point I will let the words from Helen's blog speak for her.

Friday, September 26, 2008
<u>First posting and background to date....</u>

For those of you who have not been in the loop, I'll add a little background here. I was diagnosed with breast cancer July 28 and had a meeting with a surgeon July 31. The decision from that meeting was a mastectomy, which was done Aug. 18. As you can tell from the dates, I was swept into a 'different stream' of the river of life and faced with decisions and experiences that were shocking. However, God met me and gave me His assurance that He would be with me in this experience. The day after I found out that the lump was malignant – and not a cyst as I was expecting – the verse of the day in my devotional book reminded me that the Lord my

God holds my right hand and tells me, Don't be afraid; I will help you. That has certainly proved to be the case – the help has come from many different hands and many prayers have been offered on my behalf, providing a strength and a peace of mind that have sustained me through this and continue to do so.

The next step was to get assigned to an oncologist, at either the London Regional Cancer Centre or the Windsor one. I asked to be submitted to both and requested a specific doctor in Windsor whose name kept popping up in various places. When I went to see my surgeon for the follow-up appointment on Sept. 2, the news was not good – tumour was 4.3 cm, Grade 3, and they had removed 27 lymph nodes, 24 of which were 'positive'. I heard later that afternoon that I had an appointment in London on Sept. 30 (with another good oncologist) but I asked them to keep trying with Windsor. Two days later I received a call telling me I had an appointment in Windsor the next Monday, Sept. 8, with the doctor I had requested. I felt that that was another answer to prayer.

And so, my new life began...when I went to see the doctor in Windsor, she laid out a schedule of chemo to be delivered every two weeks instead of the usual three. In order to be able to keep to this schedule, I would also need a shot to keep my white blood cell count up. In addition, I was offered a chance to apply to be part of a clinical trial for a new drug because of the type of tumour that I had – triple negative (not positive for either of two hormone receptors or HER2/neu) – lots of new terms to learn ! This chemo schedule would be followed by 6 weeks of radiation. This is a very aggressive plan, because of the number of positive lymph nodes I had and because of the grade of the tumour; I was staged at IIIC. Scary – but those promises kept coming – Sept. 4 – "He is my defender: I will not be defeated" and "Remain calm; the

Lord will fight for you". Also, I felt better and better as I recovered from the mastectomy surgery – having the tumour out of my body (and all those lymph nodes !) – seemed to be a very good thing – I could feel myself improving to the point where I felt I was almost lying about having cancer. My sister had the best line – "she's not sick; she just has cancer." And that's pretty well how I felt, too.

Then the various tests began – phone rings – "You are scheduled for a *** at ***" – no question of whether or not it is convenient – one day we had to be at the Chatham hospital for 7:30 for a heart scan then at the first Windsor hospital for 11:00 to sign papers to be admitted to the clinical trial and at a second Windsor hospital for 12:30 to have my 'port' installed for the delivery of my chemo (no IV needed). Left that hospital at 5:00 and went straight to Red Lobster for a restorative supper.

So that brings the story up to date for this past week and that will be another entry.

This surgery brought us into a new phase of our lives together. For years I had teased Helen that she was no longer the girl I married, after an appendectomy, a hysterectomy, a gall bladder removal and even the removal of her wisdom teeth. I joked that she was leaving a trail of unnecessary parts behind her. This surgery was different. Our society is obsessed with the bodies of women, and sets great store by big boobs, small waists, and rounded butts. Women, especially young women, will do almost anything to achieve the image that supposedly appeals to men. They will go under the knife for appearance altering surgeries, they will exhaust themselves at gyms trying to run off that last few ounces of weight, they will starve themselves and many in the tween and teen years especially, wind up with eating disorders. This is not to say that men do not have this same vanity and take many of the same steps. It just seems to be more prevalent in women. This surgery that Helen was having, unlike all of her previous surgeries was visible, not hidden inside her body with only scars showing on the outside. This was a blow to her image of womanhood, and was very difficult decision. In the end, her desire to live outweighed her vanity, and she agreed to the mastectomy.

The surgery went well. Helen spent two days in hospital, and then came home to recuperate. She had a drain in her chest wall that was to remove fluids that built up after the surgery. A home care nurse was assigned to her, and this lady came every other day to empty the contents of the drain bottle, record its appearance and volume and then re-attach the bottle. This nurse also attended to the healing of the surgical area. About a week after her surgery, Helen was up and about again. Her surgery was on Tuesday

August 18th, 2008. Her 63rd birthday was on August 23rd, the end of that week. Our children had all come home to celebrate the birthday, bringing their spouses, girlfriends, children for the weekend. Steve brought his family, which now included a little girl, Lily, for two weeks. They booked a cottage at a provincial park on the shores of Lake Erie, and were able to have their own private time as a family, but to share most evenings with us. They actually came for the week before Helen's surgery, so Helen had lots of grandma time to pump up her regenerative systems.

As Helen noted above, the actual tumour when removed, was 4.3 cm in diameter, and of 27 lymph nodes removed, 24 were malignant showing that the disease had already started to spread from the breast. We started down an educational path whereby we learned much about this disease, far more than we would have wished.

Breast cancers are sorted into varying designations of severity. They are classified as type I, type II, type III or type IV. Type IV is always considered a terminal illness. With the three lesser types, some hope of recovery exists. Within type III, there are classifications of A, B, and C, each again increasing in severity. Helen's tumour was designated at type III C, just short of a type IV. This brought us to a very intensive and aggressive treatment program which I will talk about in the next chapter.

I need to speak to husbands at this point. When Helen received her diagnosis and went through the surgery, this was OUR fight. We were going to tackle this disease together. We had promised years back to support each other in good and bad times, in sickness and in health, and this became my time to honour that commitment. I was horrified when Helen's oncologist told us that breast cancer is often the cause of a marriage breakup; that husbands demand a divorce because the wife has been disfigured and is now not up to standard. I could hardly believe this. This was the woman I loved with all my heart, and she was fighting a disease, and she needed me, and the thought of discarding her never entered my mind.

Instead, I focused on looking at various traits, her eyes, her smile, her laugh, her accomplishments, the way former students looked up to her and stayed in touch with her. I made a point, at least once a day, although not limited to once, to tell her how beautiful she was – how much I loved her and how much I was looking forward to years together after we whipped this disease.

I mentioned earlier that I had started a tradition in Bible College of purchasing rose corsages for her. In all of the years of our marriage I never stopped that. When she was in school, and I was bouncing around the world in my work, on a completely random basis, not tied to any special anniversary or birthday or valentine's day, or whatever, she would get paged to come to the office of the school. When she arrived, there waiting for her was a rose corsage. She would pin it on and return to her classroom, where her students would ask what the flower was for. "Oh, my husband is in Brazil, (or Germany, or Korea, or France or some other place,) and he was thinking about me" would be her reply. After her retirement, I did not have the opportunity of the subtlety of having flowers sent to her school, but often I would pick up a single long stem red rose and lay it on her pillow for her to find when she went to bed. Occasionally I would substitute some sensuous hand made chocolates from a local *Chocolatier* instead. Usually only two or three but just enough to let her know she was loved.

The bottom line as we say, was that I went out of my way to make sure she knew she was loved by me, and that she was still beautiful in my eyes, despite the results of her surgery. Her surgery also had an effect, at least from her perspective, on our more intimate life.

Like many couples in the mid sixties, our sex life was not the joyful romp it had been when we were in our twenties and thirties, but we still enjoyed the feel of our bodies next to each other, and the warmth and love that flowed between us, as God designed us, just lying under the sheets together, arms around each other and drifting off to sleep in that fashion. After her mastectomy, it was extremely difficult for Helen to come to me because she felt "damaged." Six weeks passed from her surgery, until the first night that she could take off her robe and let me see her naked. As she did so, she had such a look of apprehension and fear on her face wondering how I was going to judge her that I was the one that burst into tears. When I saw the scar where her breast had been, and almost felt the touch of the scalpel that had removed it, I hurt and hurt for her. I was very angry at this disease that had caused my beautiful wife to have to go through this. She crawled into my bed and we wrapped our arms around each other and bawled like a couple of children, and so drifted off to sleep. I had no words for her that did not sound artificial, but she truly looked as beautiful to me as she had on our wedding night, and I became even more attentive to be sure that she knew that, and most of all, that she believed it.

One additional lesson that I had to learn in the weeks and months after her surgery, was to let her maintain her independence, and not to smother her. Helen was a fiercely independent woman, combined with a love of cooking. Since I also am a bit of a chef, I thought after her surgery that I could show my love by taking over the kitchen and fixing all of her meals. Wrong ! One day when I pressed too far, she looked at me with fire in her eyes, and said "you are not going to make an invalid out of me." In my desire to be helpful, I had, in her eyes, started to treat her as if she was incapacitated, and was robbing her of all of the enjoyment that she got in the kitchen. I had to learn, day by day, to make myself available if she asked for my assistance, but to stay out of her way if she did not want my help. Trust me guys, this is a very fine balance, but an extremely important balance.

Often in her blog, Helen makes reference to cutting the grass. We have approximately one acre of grass to cut, and we have a capable John Deere tractor with which we do it. Helen loved bouncing around on the tractor, looking at the trees and her flower beds and the squirrels running out of her way, the birds and the smell of the fresh mown grass, and wanted to cut it often. I want to make it clear that I was not expecting her, in her condition to be walking around behind a hand lawn mower!

Chapter Four

Life with Chemo

As indicated earlier, we were about to learn more about cancer than we ever wanted to know. The oncologist to whom we were referred in Windsor, Dr. Caroline Hamm is an angel in disguise. She laid out for us what was happening in Helen's body, what the subtle variations were in cancer that led to one form of treatment or another. We learned about "receptors" in cancer tissue that could be receptors for estrogen, for example, or progesterone, or something called HER2 hormones. We learned that any one or combination of these receptors could make hormone treatment more or less effective. We also learned that Helen was "triple negative" which meant that she had none of these receptors which called for a completely different form of treatment. Above all, Dr. Hamm said "trust me. I am going to take care of you." So we did. We put Helen's life completely into Dr. Hamm's hands, while knowing Helen was still in God's hands, and looked forward to fighting this battle together.

One of the first things Dr. Hamm said to Helen was "I am going to make sure you are never sick." She prescribed a long list of medications, many to be taken before a chemo treatment, that were going to calm Helen's body, restore her white blood counts after treatment, and allow her to sleep at night. Throughout the months of treatment, Dr. Hamm's promise held true. Not once did Helen experience any vomiting or sever nausea or any of the other things that people make crude jokes about. She had confidence in Dr. Hamm, she did what she was told to do, took the medications she was told to take, and approached this whole regime with a determination to conquer.

At the outset of her chemo treatment, Helen was told that she might be able to be a participant in a clinical trial for a drug called Avastin, used for treatment of other forms of cancer, being considered for the treatment of breast cancer. The goal of the Avastin, as I understood it, was to reduce the blood flow to any rapidly growing group of cells, and thus prevent any new tumours from growing. To be included in this trial, Helen had to be a triple negative candidate, which she was, have not received any hormonal treatment, which she had not, and to be selected by a "randomization" process by a computer which arbitrarily chose people for the control group and for the test group. The day we were advised that Helen had been selected to actually receive the treatment, and not some form of placebo, we celebrated like we had won the world's largest lottery. In some ways we had. The inclusion in this clinical trial introduced us to "Krista" another angel in disguise at the Windsor Regional Cancer Centre. She became our guide through the year long process of the trial. After a warm welcome from the two receptionists, Amy and Pam, Krista was the first person to meet us in the examination area. She had a questionnaire that she had to complete with each visit, directed us to where we had to be in sequence – lab for blood work, then the doctor's office, then the chemo suite, and so on. She ran interference for us to ensure that events happened efficiently and as swiftly as possible, all the while exuding a warm, comfortable personality and radiant smile.

And so began a regular commute between Chatham and Windsor. In May of 2008, I had purchased a brand new car, in anticipation of Helen's second retirement, for all of the road trips we were going to make together. Little did I know that our road trips would be the same 50 mile stretch of asphalt between Windsor and Chatham. However, we had a safe, warm, comfortable car with the latest in traction and anti-skid controls for Canadian winters, and an enjoyable satellite radio that let us select songs from the 50s and 60s which we often sang along with on our drive.

One interesting, but not unexpected side effect of the chemo was that Helen lost all of her hair. That was when I discovered that she had a perfect head ! It was proportionately shaped, smooth, round and not a wrinkle in sight. Without losing my hair, but just running my fingers over the topography of my scalp, I am confident that without hair I would look like the north end of a southbound elephant. Helen on the other hand looked perfect. Throughout our marriage, I had often coaxed her to wear hats, without success. Now there was a reason to go find jaunty little caps, berets, fedoras and whatnot, combined with scarves, knitted caps and so on. She looked fantastic. I shot dozens of pictures of her in her various forms of plumage, teased her about billiard balls, and loved her even more if that was possible. She acquired a brunette wig the colour of her own hair, which looked so natural, that had I not known, I would have never thought it to be a wig.

When she completed that portion of her chemo treatment, her hair slowly came back in – the most gorgeous silver colour with charcoal highlights ! Turns out that Helen and her hairdresser had been augmenting her natural beauty with some chemical help that I never realized. Helen and I used the same hairdresser, and about two weeks before her death we were both getting a trim, and Brenda our hairdresser commented on the beautiful, natural silver colour, and speculated that it would be impossible for her to artificially create such a look. Helen commented

"If I had know what colour it really was, and how much everyone seems to like it, I would have stopped colouring it years ago." To which Brenda replied "Well I'm really glad that only occurred to you now and not years ago."

SATURDAY, SEPTEMBER 27, 2008
Update for week of Sept. 22 - 26, 2008

Tues. - had to go a day early for my CAT scan in Windsor - interesting experience but no pain involved!

Wed. - had to go for my regular Dr. visit - she promised me no nausea or vomiting and wrote out a shopping list of meds to get filled at the pharmacy - filled a whole little brown paper bag when I picked it up yesterday. Also found out that afternoon that I have been admitted to the experimental group for the research drug ! Will receive that over the course of a year - will slow to 3 week intervals when I'm done the main ones. This also means that my CAT scan was clear, I think - at least nothing showed up that would keep me out of the clinical trial. No official word yet but it's good enough for me! So - both bone scan and CAT scan are clear = no spread, although of course it would only take one little cell floating around out there, hence the chemo + radiation to come. But it's amazingly good news.

Thurs. - first chemo day - nervous. My app't was for 9:30 - left the house about 8:00, in the cancer clinic for 9:15. Had to get some blood drawn before the chemo started - problems with that took over an hour. Some chemo meds are not mixed until you are ready for them - more time...finally started about 11:00 a.m. Each med is delivered separately and because it was the first time, slowly. The first one came in three large syringes - red liquid - known as the 'red devil' or 'red bull'. The nurse told me that my hair would start to fall out in a few days - I said that the Dr. had said 3 weeks - she said, "That's when it's

ALL gone"' Next one could just be an IV drip, 45 min (will shorten to 30) and the last one (experimental) was also IV but 90 min.(will shorten to 60, then 30 for remainder.) These meds are all delivered through my 'port', a little access thingy that was inserted into my right chest 2 weeks ago - they just clip the connector into it and I have no needle in my arm. So - it was a long day - left the clinic about 4:00, home about 5:00. But - was feeling well enough to go out briefly for supper with the teachers' group that have been meeting for over 10 years now. Drove myself and came home early but it was good to be with them. Here's the best part: I've had absolutely NO nausea or anything else - yesterday, I felt sort of heavy and worn out a bit - like my body was saying "What the heck was THAT that just happened to me??" but I took it quiet after I got home, slept well and got up this morning feeling normal again - made my breakfast, took all my pills, etc. I have to go over to the Chatham hospital this p.m. to have an injection that will help my white blood count stay up so that they can keep me on a 2-week delivery schedule for the chemo. But, I feel GREAT - compared to some of the stories I have heard, etc. I am doing extremely well.

Amy is here - came down last night and will be here until Sun. I think. Nice to have the company - I should get sick more often !! ;-)

So - I continue to float on the river of prayers that are being offered on my behalf and I am at peace.

Fri - needed a diversionary tactic so went shopping in the afternoon with Amy and also attended a training session to be a Deputy Returning Officer for the upcoming election... see ? I am REALLY doing OK !

Wednesday, October 1, 2008
Reality intrudes !!

Well, now I realize what the steroids were doing ! And also what the doctor meant when she said that there would be a 'crash' after I was finished with them. Those of you who have been down this road must have been waiting for the other shoe to drop.

I went to a cancer conference on Saturday with David and Amy (daughter) and heard several interesting people, including my own oncologist who talked about research in cancer treatment and how recent some of the drugs are. That was very beneficial, especially for Amy. It was to be a full day conference, but I started 'declining' after lunch and we left. The 'flu-like' days began then and continued until about Tues. morning...woke up still feeling rotten but then, like the weather, things began to clear mid-morning and I started feeling like a 'human bean' again. So - now I know what to plan for. Returned all the election materials yesterday, with apologies - there's no way I can do that. Felt well enough to get groceries in the afternoon and am feeling even better today. Tomorrow is a regular blood check here in Chatham and that will be it for this week.

Also realized that we will not be going out of town for Thanksgiving, based on my 'down days' and that whatever happens will have to happen here. Fortunately, there are 'guest chefs' in the family who are more than able to help out.

So - hope I gave some of you a good laugh ! I'll figure out how to do this eventually!

Post a Comment On: <u>Helen's Journal</u>
Dan & Leona said...

We are not usually "first" for much of anything, but maybe we are the first to comment. We just want to remind you that you are in our daily prayers. Isaiah 40:29 "He giveth power to the faint; and to them that have no might He increaseth strength'"

Love, Dan & Leona

Wednesday Oct. 8 - End of First Cycle

Today is the last day of Cycle One of my chemo, so I am just going to catch you up on the events since last Wednesday. Basically, I have felt really well, and there are no steroids involved this time! Last Wednesday, I felt well enough to do quite a bit of cooking and have a nice stock of single-serving foods in the freezer - risotto, soup, casserole, etc. Thursday and Friday, we were able to go out in the evening, and to a restaurant for supper on Fri. I still have to be careful what I eat, because the chemo attacks any fast-growing cells in your body and that includes the linings of mouth, throat and stomach. As part of that, my voice got 'funny' - sounded like I had laryngitis - and my taste was off. Perhaps I can use that as an indicator - when I sound odd, I can expect things to taste differently.

That was only a few days in the middle of last week. By Friday, I was pretty well back to normal and I have had several very nice days this week. We decided to make a quick trip to Kitchener-Waterloo on Sunday and had a visit with Amy, Mike and Lian which was very enjoyable. (I still have to rest in the afternoons - keeps me going for the rest of the day.)

The next hurdle will be when my hair leaves. That should be any time in the next week. Apparently, there comes a day when it starts coming out in chunks - just having lots of single hairs around on my pillow now - and I have been advised to have the remainder 'buzzed' once that happens. This will include loss of eyebrows and eyelashes, too - something that I am struggling with. However, I have purchased a really nice wig (not the one I brought back from Windsor) and have a collection of hats and scarves to use. I'm just not much of a hat person - although this is one of the positives for David, who has wanted me to wear them for years ! - and trying to make a scarf look nice is usually one of the things that reduces me to bad language pretty quickly - but, hey! Practice makes perfect ! The VON [Victorian Order of Nurses] sponsored a 'Look Good, Feel Better' workshop here on Monday and I went to that. I came home with a box of 'loot' and several good ideas on what to do about the eyebrow/eyelash problem. It's only for Oct. - Feb., so it's not such a big deal and I have to keep perspective here. I was speaking recently to a good friend whose son has 6 months left of a 30-month chemo regimen; what have I got to feel bad about ?

So, overall, I had 3 'bad days' - Sat. noon - Tues. noon - and the rest of the time I was able to eat, sleep, cook, read, knit, live life and carry on as usual. We'll see if that continues as I am exposed to these chemicals over and over. (3 more doses of this kind and then 4 of the second). And I'll know to watch out for those steroids from now on !

I'll close with an experience from Monday. I went across town to the VON workshop that morning and in the afternoon, I went out for groceries. In the grocery store, I met a friend and we talked about my situation (as well as some other things!) and I mentioned that I was staged at 3C - second-last worst - but not 4 !! As I left the parking lot, I was overcome by the potential of that stage and was in tears - maybe I am just crazy here to be so confident that God is in this with me and taking me through this. I got home, parked (this involves turning and braking several times to back it in) and went in the house (didn't say anything to David about what I had been thinking). Half an hour later, he went out to move my car to use the trailer and when he put his foot on the brake, the brake line broke and the pedal went right to the floor ...fluid all over the driveway. Now, you may not look at it this way, but I took that as a very definite answer to my distress; I am being looked after and protected in some very practical ways and I will get through this, by His grace.

I hope your day goes well, wherever you are, and that you are also aware of God's blessing in your life.

Sunday, October 12, 2008
Yeah, McNaughton Eagles !!

Last Friday, October 9, my staff at McNaughton Avenue Public School decided to hold a Breast Cancer Awareness Day and to do something in support of me. They all wore pink and got to school in time for a group photo at 8:45. Once the picture was developed, they put it on a large pink Bristol board and all signed it. When I arrived for lunch, there was cake, pink balloons and LOTS of hugs. It was extremely encouraging. They also went together with the staff at the Regional Centre next door to raise $450 (at last count) for research. This was also great news, since I have been able to be part of a clinical trial and my oncologist is in charge *of research at the Windsor Regional Cancer Centre.*

They are such a great group; leaving them in 2007 was a hard thing to do, when I retired. It was a bonus to have a few months back with them last spring.

Thank you, McNaughton, for all your encouragement; you have no idea how much this means to me.

Wednesday, October 15, 2008
<u>Cycle 2 / Thanksgiving</u>

We were in Windsor for 8:00 a.m. Thursday, Oct. 9 for the second cycle of chemo - an interesting exercise for two retirees ! Anyhow - made it in good time and things went much better - I knew more what to expect and it wasn't as unnerving when the administering nurse put on safety glasses and double gloves before she started the chemo! Thank goodness again for my little port - it makes it so simple. We were able to go out for a late lunch before returning to Chatham. Friday was a good day - I made pumpkin pies and tarts for the weekend - but Saturday wasn't so nice. However, Amy had arrived Friday evening and Mike and Lian arrived Saturday afternoon and between them we had a nice Thanksgiving dinner Saturday night. We all enjoyed the meal although David was overtaken by a massive head cold which kind of derailed things for him. Visitors left after lunch on Sunday and things were quiet after that.

So far, I haven't had any days of 'flu-like symptoms' this time - no nausea at all for which I am very thankful. I have to just park myself a couple of times during the day and read or just lie down for a while but that's really all that is happening to me. Things should start to improve now again as I move into the second week of this cycle. Again, I am very thankful for this.

Other signs are a creaky voice - no way I could run a classroom ! - and falling hair. I look like a shedding dog - every comb-through brings a handful of hair with it...I now look like one of those little old ladies whose scalp you can see through their hair. Time to start with the hats, scarves and nice wig that I have accumulated. Unfortunately, I have rediscovered that I don't like the feeling of anything tight on my head - but that's the breaks, I guess. More practice !!

Thank you again for your prayers for me - they support me continually on a daily-life basis and I am able to just keep on doing my thing.

Thursday, October 16, 2008
<u>Hair Today - Gone Tomorrow !!</u>

Well, yesterday I reached the 'no hair' part of the journey. I had been shedding like a dog in the spring since about Saturday - every comb-through resulted in a handful of loose hair. I was getting very patchy - looked like a little old lady with the skull showing through what was left. So I called my dear hairdresser who has looked after me for 11 years now and went to finish the job. She buzzed what was left off, pretty much, and I am now ' down to the wood'. Quite different in appearance but feels much better - and cooler. I was pleased to discover that I have a nice-shaped head and that my ears don't stick out !! Who knew ??

It wasn't as bad as I had been thinking it would be. It's just quite a change for everyone else - I don't have to look at myself unless I'm passing a mirror but everyone else gets the full benefit.

I have also been discovering just how much heat leaves your body through your head - you hear these things but then you get to experience them. I tried wearing a little knit cap at home after I got back but I had to take it off because I was just melting. So I think around the house I will just be 'au naturel'. Don't be surprised if you drop in for a visit !

I also took my nice, new wig to my hairdresser and she styled it to look a lot like my own hair so I have another good option - plus the hats and scarves that I have bought. Until the weather turns colder, though, I'm not sure how much I'll need them.

So - that's the latest ! Regular blood check-up today - second week of cycle is starting - my voice is coming back and I am starting to sound like myself again - it should be back by tomorrow - starting to get used to the pattern of all of this.

Thank you again for your prayers, which are what keeps me going.

Post a Comment On: <u>Helen's Journal</u>
Pastor Gord said...

Hi Helen,

Welcome to the world of 'blogging'! Just sending you our prayers for restored health (and hair!) as you continue with treatment. I hope David is feeling better too. I'll be in *touch, and try and get out to see you next week.*

Gord

Evelien said...

Hi Helen,

So good to hear you are doing well considering the circumstances of your life. I consider the loss of hair a badge of honour for the courageous battle you're fighting against cancer. You are in my prayers and thoughts each day.

Evelien

Gail said...

Hi Helen,

I just found your blog and wanted to let you know that you are an inspiration to everyone who reads it. You are in our prayers and thoughts every day.

Gail

Friday, October 24, 2008
<u>Catching up - Oct. 16 - 24</u>

Greetings - I didn't want to bore you with an overload of information but apparently I have gone too far in the opposite direction and have not posted as frequently as some would like. So - I will give you a big update now and try to be on more frequently in the future.

Thurs. Oct. 16 *- regular blood work app't. at the Chatham hospital; I also called Windsor before I left to report some side effects that were happening to me - listed in the section that says 'Call your doctor if this happens'. Returned home to a voicemail that said 'Doctor will see you either today before 2:00 p.m. (not possible at that point) or at 8:30 a.m. Friday'....so, Friday it was.*

Fri. Oct. 17 *- another early morning trip to Windsor. Practiced wearing scarf and nice cap instead of wig. Turned out that the chemo meds had irritated a 'pre-existing condition' and*

I came home with even more pills. David is still suffering from a horrible chest cold, so he went back to bed and I did laundry in preparation for a very special trip on the weekend.

Sat. & Sun. Oct. 18,19 *- I was able to go away for the weekend with a very special group of friends, a teachers group who have been meeting for supper once a month for over 10 years. Twice a year, at least, we are able to go away overnight. This trip was up to Huron County on the eastern shore of Lake Huron and the fall colour was gorgeous. Craft Fair in Grand Bend, lunch in Bayfield and then on to our overnight destination, a lovely old farmhouse that belongs to the family of one of the group. I had to have a nap by that time but the girls took care of me. We bring dinner and breakfast and stay in overnight, once we get there. It's so good to be able to just catch up with each other's lives. We had a memorable evening, filled with good food and lots of glorious music. I worked up* *enough nerve somewhere during the evening to do an 'unveiling' of my bald head and everyone thought it was cool and that I could leave my wig off - so encouraging and loving. After a long a leisurely breakfast on Sunday, we headed back home, touring the Goderich jail (Doors Open Ontario Program of historical buildings) and doing a bit more shopping on the way.*

Mon. Oct. 20 *- work day around the house - 4 bags of garbage to the dump, made a turkey pie and a big pot of turkey pumpkin rice soup - more little containers of frozen goodness for the 'off days'. As you can see, these are my 'good days' and I am making the most of them.*

Tues. Oct. 21 *- day trip to Kingsville with 2 friends to visit another friend who has moved there - great times again had by all - 'unveiled' again - everyone is cool with it - so helpful when I feel that I look so different...but I do have a nicely shaped head and flat ears ! Later that night, I had my first Skype conversations with my* *two children in Kitchener and my children and grandchildren in Texas - more with wig/without wig viewings...everyone agrees that 1) my hairdresser did an exceptionally good job on my wig and 2) that wigless is not as bad as expected. So - we are all coping with that pretty well. David had had a doctor's appointment this morning for an annual physical and came home with a massive anti-biotic prescription - 1/ 500 mg. pill 3 times a day, so between the pills and the cold (bronchial viral infection) he folded pretty early.*

Wed. Oct. 22 - *lots of little jobs - formalized my Leave of Absence from the Occasional Teaching List for the rest of this school year, ordered my meds from the Windsor pharmacy so that they are ready for tomorrow, went to my old school for a visit for lunch and to thank them for their day in support - pink picture day - Oct. 10, etc and - drum roll - interviewed a cleaning lady in the afternoon who will start cleaning my house on my chemo days for 3 hours so that*

I can come home to a nice, clean house !!! A little treat for me. David's antibiotics are working - can see improvement already but he rested all day again today.

[As I look through Helen's notes again, I am touched by the fact that in the middle of her chemo treatments, most of her concern was for me and helping me to get well]

Thurs. Oct. 23 - *Chemo # 3 - in Windsor for 8:15, at lab for 8:30, picked up prescriptions 8:50, waited for dr.'s app't until 9:30ish - my Dr. was away, so saw another one - approved for chemo - then waited and waited - seemed to take longer than I remembered - didn't get called in until almost 11:00 (volunteer who was supposed to get me got side-tracked), did preliminary stuff - hooked up my port, ran saline to rinse it out - didn't actually start chemo until 11:50 but was done by 2:15. Took ourselves to a nice restaurant for a late lunch before we came home - I was feeling fine, with the help of 3 steroid pills and 2* *anti-nausea ones - almost like nothing had happened. I was encouraged again by a comment from the young woman who is my clinical trial supervisor; she asks me the same set of questions every time - how is your nausea/appetite/ sleeping/mouth sores/shortness of breath/ etc. - and for me most are normal. Her response yesterday was "It's unusual for someone to have so many normals by mid-chemo". I'll take it !!!*

So there we are - caught up to TODAY !! As you can see, my second week is very good and I am able to live a pretty normal life. My voice sounds like me again and I have good energy, although I still need to lie down for a while most afternoons - but I read or just lie quietly and listen to the radio or something – don't have to sleep as much as the first week. I will try using the additional anti-nausea pills again this time after the first 3 days are done - seemed to help last time and I wasn't as 'down'. You can learn how to do almost anything.

Thank you for your prayers, which I am constantly aware of - maybe the reason for all those 'normals' - and for your cards and e-mails and phone calls, which comfort me and fill me with calm and peace - also good medicine. I appreciate your interest in my situation and your concern for me. They are more of a help than you can know. May God be with you today and may you also feel the comfort of His presence in your life in the things that are happening to you. He is always interested in His children and waiting for your call.

Post a Comment On: <u>Helen's Journal</u>
Gail said...
Hi Helen:
Glad to see that you are having so many good days. I thought you must be feeling okay when I saw you out cutting the grass this week. Hope this keeps up.
Gail

October 24, 2008 12:57 PM
Jordyn said...

> Hey Mrs. Goldsmith! I was just thinking about you a couple days ago! And I saw Ms .Gray in the mall and she filled me in on the things going on! So I thought I would catch up with you since you've known me for sooo long and since after I graduated I was never really able to get the chance to say, Thank you. For being the only teacher I've known since I was in Kindergarten that actually managed to be able to handle me all the way through to grade 8! Anyways I hope all is well. I give you all of my best wishes and hopes, I hope you are doing well! Have a good one! Lynds and Josh say Hi too! We all miss our French days with you!
> With Love,
> Jordyn

Kristyn said...

Hi Mrs. Goldsmith!

I was talking to Jordyn the other day and she was telling me about your blog that Ms. Gray told her about. I thought I'd check it out for myself and I'm happy to read that you're having many good days! Thank you for the great days of French class, I miss them a lot... I wish you happiness and health!

Kristyn

Monday, October 27, 2008

Things are going well this time -

Things have continued to go well this cycle. David and I spent a most enjoyable day Friday, just doing 'normal stuff' - went out for lunch, drove to a nearby orchard and stocked up on apples for the winter, did some grocery shopping and eventually went out for supper, too. Not a hospital in sight all day !

Saturday, I wasn't feeling quite so well, so I started adding my extra nausea pills and things settled down. David got a chance to make supper and make cheese sauce for the cauliflower - turned out really well.

Sunday, I woke up feeling well enough to go to church, so off I went and had a good visit with friends there, especially our big Adult Sunday School class. It was good to see them again and let them see how well I am doing.

Today, (Monday) has been a pretty normal day - no extra nausea meds or anything - looking forward to supper tonight. I just have to be careful not to eat too much or too quickly these days - or I am like one of those big snakes and just have to lie down for a while and digest !

Thanks again for your prayers - I appreciate them so much.

Thursday, October 30, 2008
And then again...Oct. 30, 2008

Well, things were going pretty well, all things considered, until this afternoon. This week is the 'uncomfortable week' in the cycle - don't sleep all that well, throat is tender and my voice sounds creaky, up frequently at night - all part of the chemo effects. They usually start diminishing by the second weekend and then I have 4 or 5 days of 'normal' - what I think of as my 'comfortable week'. This time I have also had a cold - thought for a long time that it was just the sinus irritation that is also a side effect of one of the chemo drugs, but it has declared itself as a cold with sneezing and coughing as well as too much nose-blowing. (I actually had it when we went for chemo last week and I was approved for the treatment.)

Today, I went for my regular blood work at the Chatham hospital and then treated myself to a visit at my former school, since I was 'all dressed up'. I had a nice visit in the staff room with quite a few people and talked with some more on the way out - medicine comes in many forms ! I felt pretty good, I thought, and others that I saw today agreed. Then, this afternoon, I got a call from the pharmacy in Windsor saying that my white blood count was 'way too low - down to 1.1 instead of 4.5 - 7 - and that my doctor was putting me on antibiotics. That was a surprise! (I get a shot 24 hours after my chemo is finished to keep my white blood cell count up.) But I am tired, when I stop to think about it. So - more pills. I hope that they work enough that I can keep on the delivery schedule and receive the next treatment on Nov. 6.

So now I will have to be more careful, wash my hands more, etc. - be more careful who I kiss !! Still up, dressed and going though, so don't think I am out for the count yet.

Thank you for your cards of encouragement - there's one in the mail almost every day - and for your ongoing prayers. I am humbled by the love and concern that so many show me.

Tuesday, November 4, 2008
<u>Just Carrying On...Nov. 4/08</u>

These are my 'good days' and I'm just enjoying them...and trying not to overdo it so that my white blood cell count can recover. We went for groceries Saturday afternoon and went out for supper that night with 'the cousins'. (David has a large group of cousins on his mother's side in the area and some of them try to get together every 6 - 8 weeks or so). Sunday, I made it to church in the morning and then in the afternoon made an apple pie, something I haven't done in a couple of years. I just had a taste for one - and there was enough pastry left over to make a blueberry pie for someone else! Desserts for the week!! Didn't do much yesterday - just a bit of junk removal...throwing out some magazines from 2000 ! Why do we think we will ever re-use some of this stuff ??

So - just putzing along, hoping my white blood cells are doing good things and that when I get to Windsor on Thursday, I will be able to have my next treatment. I am concerned that if my WBC is too low, the treatment will be delayed...and I still have this nose-blowing thing going on. Is it a cold or is it sinus irritation from the chemo? This coming treatment will be the last one of the first type and then on Nov. 20 I switch to the second kind of chemo. The first delivery of that will take 6 hours - it tends to produce allergic reactions and it is delivered slowly the first couple of times. Then still 30 min. for the clinical trial drug after that...but I will move into the room with the beds for this, so it shouldn't be too bad and I can nap if I need to.

My children all think I look good sans hair, but I tell them "Enjoy it while you can!" We have all become Skype converts in the last couple of weeks, so they have all seen me 'au naturel' and are quite complimentary in their relief. It's a scary thought, to see your mother bald. But not as scary as imagined and actually not too bad ! Interestingly enough, my hair seems to be growing back in a bit. We'll see what the second kind of chemo does; still have eyebrows and eyelashes, too.

My thought for the week has from the story of Job - God knows every detail of what is happening to me, and when He has tested me, He will purify me in the same way that gold is refined and purified by fire. The creative process is ongoing in our lives, making us into the people that God intended us to be.

Friday, November 7, 2008
Cycle # 4 starts - Nov. 7, 2008

Well, yesterday turned out just fine, after all my fussing. I called Windsor and got permission to get an extra blood test done here in Chatham on Wednesday, hoping to avoid a trip on Thursday just to find out that my white blood cells were too low for a treatment. I called Windsor Wednesday afternoon to see how things had turned out - "A nurse will call you." No call came in Wednesday, and fortunately my appointment on Thursday was at 12:30, not the usual 8:00 a.m. So I called again at 8:30 Thursday - same message. We were planning to leave by 10:00 to do some other errands on the way, and when I hadn't heard anything by 9:30, I called the pharmacy and requested my usual meds for a treatment day and decided I was going, regardless! Nobody had told me not to ! Also ran around getting things cleared and cleaned for my cleaning lady, who was coming that morning...which is why I missed the little blinking light on the answering machine.

We drove to Windsor and I followed ordinary procedure - start at the lab and have more blood drawn - getting pretty good at that by now! Then upstairs for the doctor's appointment and approval for chemo. Had to wait for the lab results, which were great! My white blood counts were right back up to normal range! Apparently, that Neulasta shot that I am also on works more in the second week than the first and was responsible for my rebound. Live and learn. So, after that it was just normal procedure all the way. I had a very interesting chat with the nurse who was delivering my first type of chemo - it has to be injected into the port line from 3 big syringes and takes 30 - 45 min. She had just returned from her 5th Ironman competition - 2.5 mi. swim, bike ride equal to Windsor - London and then a full 26 mi. marathon run. She has children in university, so I'd say she was in her 40's. I was IMPRESSED! Life is full of interesting people.

We left Windsor about 5:30 and drove home. I took David out for supper to thank him for all his faithful driving and support for me. He's been there for me for all of this - I haven't had to do any of it alone. Doctor's visits, surgery, driving back and forth to Windsor, listening to me fuss and fret, reminding me of various doctor comments, waiting patiently out in the waiting room for hours while I have treatments, so many things. One dinner certainly doesn't cover it all, but it also meant neither of us had to cook ! We ended the day thankful for all that had turned out well.

When we got back to the house, I checked for phone messages...and got a message that had come in at 9:31 in the morning (while I was renewing my meds) telling me that everything was fine and that I should come in for my treatment !

Rain was forecast for today but I am sitting here looking out the window at blue sky and white clouds, so I don't know...still a few things to do outside. We are also embarked on the project of clearing out the garage enough to get in one car for the winter...not bad for a 2-car garage! We are getting close and have thrown out a lot of junk, which will please our children, but there is more to do there, too, plus a lasagna to make today. So - will see what I can accomplish today while those steroids are doing their thing.

Hope your day goes well and that you are blessed in some way today.

Tuesday, November 11, 2008
Cycle # 4 continues...Nov. 11, 2008

Well, I was doing really well up to Sunday - went to Sunday School and Church services and out for lunch afterwards...felt good and had a good day. Monday, not so much. I aggravated a 'pre-existing condition', due to one of the anti-nausea meds I am on, and spent most of the day horizontal. Today is not a lot better and there is a list of things I had planned to do that will not happen today either. Just have to listen to my body and not push it beyond what it can handle...and try not to expire from boredom in the process ! Have even returned to watching T.V. in desperation some days - just need a time-filler that doesn't require too much effort. I've read all the books I have on hand, for those of you who know what a reader I am - you can only read them so many times. I have learned to order through Amazon but there are limits for that, too - there are stacks of books all around my bedroom as it is. (We have a good library in town, but you have to get there, and look around, and decide on books, etc. More effort than I can manage right now.)

So - just feeling sorry for myself today - you see that I am not always 'up' ! It will pass, as it has done before, and this is the last time that I have to deal with the effects of these first two drugs. We'll see what the next kind brings - I hear it's not as nauseating and that might help me with this other issue, too. Poor bodies!

What we do to them !! And they still keep going, healing themselves as they go.

Thanks again for your prayers.

Thursday, November 13, 2008
Cycle # 4 - Halfway - Nov. 13, 2008

Wednesday dawned a better day and today has been really good. Things settled down for me and I have been feeling much better than on Monday and Tuesday. I guess I just have to accept the fact that there are going to be a couple of bad/unpleasant days regardless of what steps I take to avoid them. But I'll try again next cycle and see what I can do to avoid as much as possible!

Today I was able to go shopping at several locations and go out for lunch with teaching friends I haven't seen for a while. I went out for lunch on Wednesday also but I was moving much more slowly; I get sore on the bottoms of my feet and the palms of my hands as a result of one of the chemo meds. I also had a great visit on Wednesday afternoon with dear friends whom I have known for over 40 years (how can that be ?), who live some distance away but who were passing through on their way to Windsor. So good to be able to have time with all these people who have been part of my life for a long time; it is a different kind of medicine. And guess what ? I'm going out for lunch tomorrow, too ! More time with good friends and good food ! And even better, my son is coming from Texas for the weekend and the two kids who live in Kitchener-Waterloo will come as well, so I will see three out of four of them, plus a lovely girlfriend from K-W, on the weekend. What wonderful medicine that will be !!

So, back on keel and doing OK. Thanks again for your prayers on my behalf. I am always conscious of their uplifting strength.

Wednesday, November 19, 2008
Update - Nov.19, 2008

I've had a wonderful second week of this cycle - have felt like a normal, healthy person and have lived my life like that. Thanks be to God!

Friday: Went out for lunch as planned (terrific time), came home for my nap and then got supper ready for the incoming - son from Texas, daughter from Kitchener, husband from Toronto (homemade lasagna, a family tradition).

Saturday: Shopping with son and daughter in the afternoon, second son and girlfriend arrive in snowstorm - it's only November! - with new TV for us; joint present to get us into the 21st C. Later, we all go out for supper and have a great meal and a good visit. We're all about good food!

Sunday: Late breakfast because everyone is leaving later; attend CKSS high school gym rededication to honour a retiring teacher and all kids have a good visit with former teachers they haven't seen for 10 years or more. It was so good to have our kids home for the weekend; their energy and love fill the house. I appreciate their care and just their presence - they've become pretty interesting people and they're just fun to have around. They all went home in a snowstorm again but arrived safely at their home ports.

Monday: General housework - still working on that garage ! Also get out for lunch - again - this time with my dear husband!

Tuesday: Snow and cold weather have finally killed off the last of the flowers in the beds closest to the house; I can now rip out all the remnants without feeling like I have been personally responsible for their end. And - I get invited out for lunch with my husband again ! I'm on a roll !

Wednesday: Over to our GP's office before 9:00 for a flu shot and general errands after that - including breakfast out - just to make a change. By suppertime, there is a car parked in the garage !! Success at last!! Thanks to those who offered to help but it was too grungy and fiddly - had to do it on our own.

Tomorrow/Thursday: Start the second kind of chemo - have to be IN WINDSOR for 8:00 a.m. Because it is the first delivery of this kind, it will be 6 hours, followed by 30 min. of the clinical trial drug. I usually don't get started the chemo part of the day until about 10:30 - 11:00, so it's going to be a long day. However, it will get shortened each time I have it after tomorrow, if it follows the previous patterns. I have learned how to live with the first kind of chemo; not sure what will change now with the second. Time will tell.

So, you see, I had a great week. I feel normal, I look normal (except for the hair - and if I'm wearing my wig, you might not even notice that) and I can live my normal life. (I was going to say I act normal, but that would leave me open to many spurious comments, so I will leave that out!) I need to rest in the afternoon for about an hour but that's it. I am so thankful; I feel so blessed. I think it is largely the result of all the prayers that are constantly being offered up for me and I thank each of you who are taking the time to do that. This may all change tomorrow with the new chemo, but I will know that recovery and return are possible and that will help me deal with whatever tomorrow brings.

Friday, November 21, 2008
How Thursday went (Nov. 20, 2008)

Just a quick update here to tell you that the day went very well, as far as any reaction to the new type of chemo. It can produce an allergic reaction and I was a little concerned - but they give Benadryl through the IV before the chemo as well as the steroid to help control that. I have had no reaction at all to this point and feel just my normal self. I have 3 days of supplemen-

tary meds - antinausea, etc. - so we'll see what happens when they are finished. I was warned about aching joints 36 hours after the chemo that should last for another 36 hrs. as well as tingling on palms of hands and soles of feet, because this type attacks nerves and can cause permanent damage. I sat for a while with both hands in cups of ice water to reduce circulation in my fingers during the chemo admin., so that not as much of it would get to my fingertips. Kind of hard to read and turn the pages...but I just alternated hands eventually.

The day itself was long, though. We were up by 6:00 and left the house by 6:40, arriving in Windsor before 8:00 - I was actually in the lab by then. Got blood drawn, was one of the first ones in to see the doctor - and then found out that my MUGA scan (heart video) had not been sent from the Chatham hospital. Had to wait at least 30 min. for that, sitting in the doctor's examining room . Nice visit with the doctor when that arrived - we are all pleased with how well I am doing - talked about my CT scan and the fact that it is clear - no spread of cancer to any internal organs! Good news ! (I had heard this before but had not had a chance to discuss it with my own doctor.) On the way from Doctor's office to chemo waiting room, I barely had time to go to the washroom before they were calling me in for chemo - looking good, time wise ! However, when they were setting me up, we ran into a big problem. My port wouldn't run cleanly to their satisfaction. It is always flushed out with saline and then they withdraw a little blood, to make sure it is open and that the chemicals will flow in properly from the chemo. You can have some serious problems if there are any leaks. Anyhow - they couldn't get any blood to come out due to a protein buildup or something, and it took them from 10:00 - 11:45 and several different procedures to finally get it open - plus some fervent prayers on my part ! Chemo didn't get started until 12:00 and I'm thinking I'm going to be there till 7:00 or so - 6 hrs. for the first chemo plus 30 min. for the clinical trial drug plus flushing the line every time they have to change IV bags. But a little 'magic' was performed somewhere along the line - helped by me not having any bad reaction to the chemo I think - vitals were checked every 15 min. for the first hour or so - and I walked out at 4:45 ! We stopped for dinner on the way home and were back in town about 7:00 p.m. Long day but it could have been longer !

So - went well - everything's cool - we'll see what the weekend brings. Thanks for your prayers.

Update Nov. 27, 2008

Happy Thanksgiving to any south-of-the-border readers today! I hope you have a great time with family and friends, in spite of the economic shakings we are all experiencing.

This week on the new chemo has followed much of the pattern of the first type. As long as I am on my supplementary meds after the treatment, I feel OK but when they stop, then I have a reaction to that and then I am OK again. So, Friday, Saturday and most of Sunday I was able to do the things I normally do - shopping for groceries, garbage to the dump, make it to Sunday School, go out for coffee, etc. Sunday afternoon things start to slide and Monday wasn't very good - actually spent the day in my jammies, which is rare. However, by Monday afternoon, things started to improve, and Tuesday was better - went out for supper and had a good visit with a long-time friend. Yesterday I went to get my wig re-styled and several other errands. I missed my afternoon rest and that wasn't a good idea. I'll have to make sure I get it today - or plan to be in bed by 8:00 p.m. like I was last night !

I have noticed that this type of chemo doesn't make my nose run like a tap but I do seem to be more tired and my fingers feel like I have extra skin on them. I will definitely have to put them in that ice water again at the next treatment. I don't want to lose feeling permanently.

So - just truckin' along, doing what I can, starting to think about Christmas and getting the house ready for that. Thank you again for your prayers.

Update - Wednesday, Dec. 3, 2008

Here we are at the end of the fifth cycle - off to Windsor tomorrow for my sixth treatment ! I'll be finished chemo in a month - Jan. 2. Hard to believe! Anyhow - my take on this second type of chemo is that 1) it makes me more tired that the first kind 2) the skin on the palms of my hands is drier and peeling - have to use LOTS of really good hand cream 3) I don't get 'chemo voice' so much with it and there is less nose-blowing although my throat is still fairly sensitive and 4) I seem to get a little more emotional with it - although that may just be part of the overall process. So - better, overall.

I was able to attend a social event last night out of town and made it to 11:00 p.m.! There's life in these old bones yet. I also had lunch with good friends yesterday- as I did with a college roommate last Saturday. I will take this kind of medicine as often as I can get it! I am blessed with many friends who take me out and cheer me up.

All in all, it's been a good cycle; I'm hoping that my body will adjust to this chemo as it seemed to with the first and that I will see less impact each time. I'm also hoping for a shorter day tomorrow and that my port will be running clear the first time !

Thanks for your prayers.

Thursday, Dec.4, 2008

It was another long day, but it went well. Up at 5:15, made breakfast and lunches, cleared the kitchen area of 'stuff' so that the cleaning lady could wash the floor - you know how that goes - set up the dog outside and left the house at 6:50. It's an interesting drive this time of year, because you start out in the dark and the highway is a moving ribbon of lights - yellow towards you, red going away, all against this black background. About Tilbury, the background starts to lighten and becomes grayish - clouds appear in the sky as darker shadows. In another 10 min., the clouds become whiter and there are patches of blue in the sky; by Windsor it is full daylight.

We arrived at the hospital just before 8:00, got a good parking place and were in the lab just after 8:00. Every second time I'm there, I have to have extra blood drawn because I'm in this clinical trial. So, in addition to the 2 tubes that are the regular draw, I have to have another 4. There's always a problem with the extra ones - no vacuum in 2 of them, so it takes longer to fill them and then the other 2 have some fluid in them which cannot get back into me, so they have to be held at a certain angle. Well, the first 2 regular ones were fine, but not so the other 4. The decision was made to get them out of my port in the treatment process.

Doctor's visit was next - she's very pleased with my progress - said I was a 'star'. Always good to hear ! We also agreed on a modification of one of my supplementary meds which should help a lot with the problems I have been having 3 or 4 days into the cycle. Then - pick up my meds at the pharmacy and wait to be called into chemo. I almost forgot to put my name in to register for the chemo!

I was called in about 10:30 and thought I was in good time. My port opened up perfectly the first time they tried it ! But then - had to get those 4 tubes of blood first, then a dose of Benadryl and a second drug which prevent allergic reaction, then a saline flush, then the steroid, then a flush, then order the chemo to be made up...

all normal practice. I think I started the actual chemo about 11:30 - 4 hr. delivery because it was only my second time and they do not want to trigger an allergic reaction. This time the Benadryl really made me sleepy, so it was no problem to sit with my hands in the ice instead of reading - I had nice little 'drifts', in and out and a very peaceful afternoon. After the Taxol, another flush and then 30 min. for the clinical trial drug, Avastin. So, actually finished about 4:20, a half-hour earlier than last week.

Of course, all the while that I am getting these treatments, David is waiting, and waiting, and waiting in the waiting room – from 10:30 until 4:20. It's a long day for him, too.

We stopped for supper on the way home at what is becoming our regular place, a diner at the corner of Manning Rd. and Essex 42. They had their hamburgers on special and it sounded good, but I was surprised to find that it was just too much meat for me - odd to discover that I just don't eat that much meat at a time any more.

We were taking the mail out of the mailbox at 6:20 - away from home almost 12 hours. The dog was glad to see us and we were glad to be back home. As David said, he got me there and back once again and on time !

I continue to feel that one of the biggest reasons that I am doing so well is the number of prayers that are offered on my behalf and I thank each one of you that is taking the time to remember me. I felt at the beginning of this whole experience that God was bringing it into my life for His purposes - one of them might be to give some of you a reason to pray again and to see His answers. One of them is definitely to show me that He is actively participating in my life and that I can trust His care for me. He is continuing to shape me into the person He intends me to be, as a potter does with clay.

Post a Comment On: <u>Helen's Journal</u>

Amanda said...

I cannot believe that you can find the goodness in everything you're going through, you are one amazing woman, and MY prayers are definitely going for you, as I'm sure that He has a very good reason. Your faith makes me have faith.

12 hours! That is such a long procedure! You obviously have more patience than most people do.

Sincerely
Amanda

Allyson said...
Bonjour Madame :)

hi, its Allyson

I've read all of your posts and it's good to see you're doing well. I miss you soooo much ! You taught me so much, and I'll never forget a word. I wish we could talk in person, but this is just as good. I have to be going now, but I would love to hear back from you, my prayers are yours, but your strength is mine. With you the impossible, is possible, and you make the non-believers, believe-- that everything will be okay.

- Allyson

Deanna said...
bonjour Madame ! :)
it's deanna !
long time no talk ! :
(i miss you, but it's good to here that things are getting better ! :)
if you want to chat here's my email :

you're always in my prayers Madame !
xoxo
deanna ! :)

Update - Friday, Dec. 12, 2008

I'm happy to report that it's been a good week - the changes that were made to my supplementary meds were good for me. It has followed the usual pattern - Fri. to Sun. were fairly normal, since I had my meds; Monday did not start off very well, since I was coming off the steroids. I was very tired in the morning - couldn't even read; just lay on my bed and listened to the radio. By suppertime I had come around enough to go out for supper (neither of us felt like cooking). Then it just gets better as I go along - went out for a Christmas dinner Tuesday, went to a funeral visitation and shopping (including groceries) Wednesday, more shopping Thursday, and today I feel pretty normal and plan on doing some Christmas baking. I go to bed a little later every night - less tired as I go along. So - that's the 'bad' week and I still have my 'good' week to go! I do seem to be adapting to the Taxol and I am thankful. The worst thing about it - and it's not a big thing at all - is that the skin on my palms and soles of my feet is very dry and tender; hard to walk some days and I have to put hand cream on every night to stop the peeling. And I have a couple of days of being tired - not much at all.

We're looking forward to Christmas and some time with some of our kids. Thanks again for your prayers - next treatment is Dec. 18 - second last ! I'm so thankful that this is going so well and I appreciate the prayers of you who have remembered me; it's one of the main reasons why I am so well.

Post a Comment On: Helen's Journal

Amanda said...

TWO MORE TO GO MADAME GOLD-SMITH! hang in there! May God bless you,

Update - Wednesday, Dec. 17, 2008

Good morning! Well, here we are at the end of cycle # 6 - going for my 7th treatment tomorrow. Things have gone really well all this second week and I have felt, one might actually say, healthy! Sleeping well without pills, eating well, doing normal stuff around the house - if it wasn't for my bald head, you'd probably not know there was anything wrong with me. Still going out for those lunches with friends, which are a type of medicine in themselves... still keeping up with meals, Christmas shopping and decorating, etc. Biggest effect of this type of chemo seems to be tiredness and dry skin on palms and soles of feet - not big but have to be dealt with. Thanks again for your prayers.

Yesterday, in a book I was reading, I came across a verse from the Bible that I hadn't thought of in a while - "And we know that all things work together for good to them that love God, to them who are the called according to

His purpose." That is not to say that everything that happens is good (like my cancer) but that God works to bring good out of the situation (like the people who are praying for me who might not have prayed in a while.) So I wait to see how this upsetting thing is going to be used to expand my life - what will grow out of this after I am through all these treatments ? Time will tell.

Post a Comment On: *Helen's Journal*

Amanda said...

Hi Mme Goldsmith,

just finished reading this blog, I'm a bit behind, but keep up the attitude Mme. Goldsmith, it can almost make me cry how people can complain everyday about little things like if their water is cold, and you're not even complaining about something this big.

I know this is one of the reason I respect you so much Madame.

Have a very merry and SAFE Christmas.

prayer and wishes like always,
Amanda

Update for Thursday, Dec. 18, 2008

We followed the usual routine yesterday - up at 5:15, out of the house about 6:45, in the parking lot in Windsor 3 minutes before 8:00 (as pointed out by my steady chauffeur!), etc. Everything went well at the lab and with the doctor's visit - she continues to be pleased with how I am tolerating the chemo - and then off to the chemo clinic. They always do a 'vitals check' - blood pressure, oxygen levels, temperature - and that's where things started to go off the rails. My first blood pressure was 163/100. I had been sitting in the waiting room for about 20 min. and had only walked about 100 ' into the clinic and laid down on the gurney - not a tremendous exertion. Protocol says I cannot receive the Avastin (the clinical trial drug) if my top number is over 150 because it's purpose is to restrict blood flow. So I tried to 'meditate/calm myself', and it came down to 138/89...better, but still not good, considering that I am already on medication to lower my b.p. Also, the Benadryl and other anti-allergic meds that I am given should relax things and help lower my b.p. I got the Taxol, my regular chemo, lying down and being quiet for the 3 hrs. that took - nice little drifts again - but when the nurse came to take my vitals again before the Avastin, I was sitting up, and my b.p. was 152/89...lying down brought it to 148.87. So the decision was made that I would skip the Avastin this trip and have it again Jan. 2. We also talked about my regular dosage of b.p. meds and increased that from 10 mg. to 15. They were very clear that it is the effect of the Avastin - 'well-documented' was the expression used - and when combined with 'a previously-existing condition', not a surprise. I will have the Avastin Jan. 2 and 15, and after that it will become a 3-week cycle, so that should also help. It will also be interesting these 2 weeks to separate out the effects of the Avastin from the other chemo - I'll maybe know better what I will be dealing with once I am only on Avastin. I also have an appointment Jan. 5 with my radiologist to set up the schedule for that part of the treatment.

So - an interesting day. We were finished chemo about 3:15 but had to wait for a new prescription for my b.p. meds so actually left the building about 4:00. We stopped for supper in Windsor and then did a bit of shopping and got gas - 69.4 !! - on the way home, so it was still about a 12-hr. day. Only one more to go !

I really have to give credit to the nurses in the chemo clinic. They are so good - professional in their approach to their responsibilities but kind and personal in their approach to the patients. I may be cared for by 2 or 3 of them in the course of a visit - one main one but the others cover over lunch or if my main one is busy with another patient. When I think that they do this every day, I am very respectful of their level of competence. I think that there are 24 places in the clinic; I think that there would be 30 - 35 people come through daily - there are morning and afternoon appointments in part of the clinic. There seem to be 8 nurses who look after all of that, plus the charge nurse. It's a busy place !

Thank you again for your prayers. I continue to do well - feeling pretty good today but I'm on my supplementary steroids and anti-nausea stuff. We'll see what Monday brings, when they are done. Regardless, it is continuing to go extremely well and I truly feel that your prayers are a big part of the reason.

VERY brief update - Tuesday, Dec. 30, 2008

We have been having a very busy Christmas - and a very enjoyable one ! As a result, I have not updated this blog. We are going out of town today as well, so I will get back to it after we return. Last chemo coming up on Jan. 2 ! Lots to tell, just no time to do a proper job. Everything is going well except my blood pressure, which is not coming down adequately. Best wishes for a Happy New Year in 2009.

Christmas 2008

Well, we had a great time, in spite of several airline mix-ups. First to arrive was my daughter from Kitchener, who came Saturday, Dec. 19 ahead of another snowstorm and two days before she had planned to come. Next, son from Seattle and lovely girlfriend, who had an unplanned overnight in Las Vegas but made it for a lasagna supper Tuesday, Dec. 23. On Dec. 24, we had a lovely evening with some of our oldest and dearest friends after the Candlelight Service at church. The phone rang while we were all munching and talking with the best news - the Texas crew were going to be able to make it after all ! Plans had changed at their end and they had tickets to fly up Christmas Day afternoon ! We were all pretty excited ! Their original plan was to overnight in Detroit and arrive early Boxing Day; actual outcome was an overnight in Chicago and arrival in time for Christmas dinner late on Boxing Day. Christmas Day evening saw the arrival of our youngest son from Kitchener and his lovely girlfriend. My sister also drove down from Ottawa on Boxing Day. So, by Boxing Day evening, we were all under the same roof, enjoying Christmas dinner at a very extended table! I was able to cook that dinner and it gave me huge satisfaction to be able to do so.

The next day, the men took over the kitchen and David cooked a wonderful French meal - fois gras, cassoulet, roast duck and crème brulée ! The ladies retreated to the hotel where most of the people were staying and had a relaxed lunch and some shopping. I went for a brief walk with my Texas grandson and helped him make and throw some snowballs - a first for him! Quite a day !

But then we got to the sad part, where people had to leave. Our Seattle son and girlfriend had to leave Sunday, Dec. 28 - had another unexpected overnight as part of their return trip and a late departure on this trip too. Our Kitchener son and girlfriend returned Monday and my sister left Tuesday morning to drive back to Ottawa. Fortunately, she had good weather both trips. The rest of us packed up Tuesday also and went to Kitchener for New Year's so we were able to have a couple more days together. We were treated to a wonderful Asian dinner at a restaurant Tuesday evening, where David presented me with a beautiful necklace, to celebrate the successful end of my chemo. Then we had twelve people at my daughter's house New Year's Eve, enjoying an amazing Laotian/Thai dinner prepared by my son's lovely girlfriend and her sister.

New Year's Day was the wrap-up - we had breakfast together and then had to leave. The Texas crew drove back to Detroit to prepare for a 7:00 a.m. flight the next day - a baby and a toddler and all the attendant baggage; they made it, too ! David and I returned home later in the afternoon and called it a day.

So, all in all, it was a wonderful time, especially because we were all together for a couple of days, because I got in lots of grandma time that I wasn't expecting and because all of our children, my lovely daughter-in-law and the great girlfriends did so much to just make it happen. I thank you all for your time in airports, time in the kitchen, time doing odd jobs around the house, time just being here. It was the best gift of all.

Jan 2, 2009 - Last Chemo Trip!

We had just returned from Kitchener the day before but we made it up by 5:30 or so and were in Windsor in the lab just after 8:00 a.m. There was a line-up - something I hadn't seen before. We were processed about 8:30 and upstairs waiting to see the doctor before 9:00 a.m. I didn't see my own doctor as she was taking a holiday, but was able to have my check-up shortly after 9:00, got my meds from the pharmacy and was called in to the chemo suite by 10:00 a.m. (My blood pressure numbers were fine all day, so we are wondering if the device I was using at home was accurate.) It was looking pretty good for an early day until they tried to get my port open...three hours later, it cleared. It was frustrating, since this had happened two cycles back as well. There is a protein build-up inside the vein and it has to be cleared out before they will administer the chemo drugs. They certainly don't want them going into the wrong location inside of me. So, the end result was that I closed the place down at 6:00 p.m. and two nurses had to wait with me to finish the procedure. A long, frustrating day - but the last one ! I will still have to go to get the experimental drug chemo until Sept. but that's only 30 min. so even if I have this port problem again it won't take so long. We left Chatham at 7:00 a.m. to be in Windsor for 8:00 a.m. and we left Windsor at 7:00 p.m. (stopped for supper) to be home for 8:00 p.m. Long day.

I return to Windsor Monday afternoon to meet my radiologist and get set up for my treatments for that - marking the location, etc. I should also be getting my schedule, so I will know when this starts and time of day, etc. That will give shape to the next two months, as I will go daily to Windsor, Monday to Friday, for 6.5 weeks. The actual treatment time isn't long, apparently, but it has to be done daily. On Jan. 15, I also get my Avastin chemo but will switch to a three-week cycle for it then. A couple of days, I will have both chemo and radiation, I guess. Then there will also be some tests again - a heart video and possibly another CT scan. I am well monitored.

And, last but not least, my hair should start growing back about the third week in January - it's already kind of growing and looks like stubble, so I'm optimistic. I imagine by Easter I will have enough to stop using my wig, or possibly sooner.

Thanks again for your prayers and your ongoing support. I wish each of you a Happy/ Blessed New Year for 2009

Sixteen weeks may seem like a long time to some. It seemed like a very long time as we were going through this period, yet looking back it seems to have passed in a heartbeat. I would drive Helen and accompany her through her steps with the lab work first, then the visit with the doctor, then to the chemo suite. While I sat with her for her first treatment, I felt in the way, and Helen seemed like she wanted to sleep, so for additional treatments I became a fixture in the waiting room. Helen would be served a lunch during the course of her treatment, but my choices were to go the hospital cafeteria, which had excellent meals, or to an in-house Tim Horton's which had only doughnuts and muffins, not their more nourishing soup and sandwiches. To leave my post in the waiting room made me feel that I was somehow abandoning Helen. I know it sounds silly, because I was not within eyesight of her anyway, but in the waiting room, I was "there."

So, for each chemo trip, Helen would pack a lunch for me in an insulated carry bag. A couple of sandwiches, some fruit, a bottle of cold water and I was set. I would take this, along with earplugs to drown out the incessant blather coming from talk shows on the waiting room TV, arm myself with a good book, and settle in for the duration. This is when I especially appreciated the volunteer ladies and men, all of whom had been impacted by cancer in their lives or in the lives of family members, as they would sit and chat with me, encourage me, offer to pray for Helen and I, and just generally keep me company.

These first two rounds of chemotherapy came to an end in January 2009, and now it was time to move on to radiation.

Chapter Five

Radiation

J anuary 5th, 2009. We are back in Windsor, and we are introduced to Dr. Khalid Hirmiz, a gentle, quiet, soft spoken gentleman who was going to bring us into the world of radiation. The first visit was only a consult, in which he described the way in which the radiation would work, its purpose and what it was supposed to accomplish, the potential effects on Helen's skin, a warning that it was a cumulative treatment, so that Helen would become more and more fatigued with each treatment, and that the impact to her skin would become more visible with each treatment, and that the effect would continue to be more evident in the first weeks following the last treatment. He explained that this was going to be a rather aggressive treatment regime, because of 27 lymph nodes removed during Helen's surgery, 24 were malignant showing that the disease was already attempting to spread, and that of course there was always the possibility of re-occurrence.

With those words, my heart sank; it felt like it was going to come out of the bottoms of my feet. I looked at Helen and her face had gone very pale, and tears were beginning to form in her eyes. I took her hand, squeezed it for a minute and just looked into her eyes, shutting the doctor out momentarily. We both knew what the other was thinking. What's this about re-occurrence? Helen is doing well. She has come through all of this chemo without being sick once. The chemo is obviously working because she lost all of her hair, and it is now just starting to grow back in.

She has beaten this disease and is on the comeback. How can you say re-occurrence?

Doctor Hirmiz realized that we were both extremely upset and hastened to assure us that this was a remote possibility and that he was going to do all within his power, his skill and the capability of his equipment to ensure that this would not happen, but re-occurrence was still a possibility. I realize in our litigious society, that doctors have to protect themselves from inconsiderate and vengeful lawsuits from angry patients and relatives, and as a result have to inform patients of all possibilities, but Helen and I left his office crushed. There were a lot of tears in the car on the return trip to Chatham, and many more that night as we cuddled in each other arms and gave way to our grief and fear.

I need to note here that Helen and I were given peace of mind from the first visit with the surgeon at the beginning of this journey, to place our trust in the medical community treating her.

We never once questioned the wisdom or direction of any of the doctors. We never sought multiple opinions or questioned the treatments laid out before us. We both believed that God was with us in this journey, and trusted Him to bring us into contact with the people He chose to treat Helen. This was difficult for our children, especially for our American daughters who were familiar with a far more intrinsic approach to medicine, with multiple referrals, multiple opinions, comparing the thoughts of one medical professional against that of another, and trying to see the path through potentially conflicting directions. At the outset, I believe that our children thought Helen and I were being naïve or too accepting of what we were told by the medical community. However at no time did they attempt to interfere, regardless of how fearful they may have been and slowly came to see that Helen and I were accepting the medical directions being given to us, not because we were apathetic, or gullible, but because we both were convinced that God was in control, that He would identify the people who should treat Helen, and that He would give them the wisdom and insight, to do what was in His plan. What a comforting feeling.

Friday, January 9, 2009
Update - Friday, Jan. 9, 2009

It's been an unusual and difficult week; I haven't been able to write about it until today, for several reasons.

On Monday, we went to Windsor to meet my radiologist and start the process for my radiation treatments. In the course of the explanation of what I would be having, the phrase 'high risk of return' was used and it somehow caught both David and I off guard and threw us 'for a loop'. It's not news - we knew I had several factors that weren't good - but I guess that I had been doing so well through the chemo that we had not thought about it for a while. I will have 25 regular radiation treatments, starting Jan. 20 (trial run Jan. 19), followed by 4 booster treatments on my chest wall, because the surgeon was only able to get a clear margin of 1 mm. instead of 1 cm. So that was one of the upsetting details to think about again this week. (I should be finished about the end of February.)

Then, I was just really affected by the chemo this time and spent a good deal of the week horizontal, on the couch or on my bed. It hasn't hit me like this since the first time in September. My fingers are numb/tingly on all the last joints - hard to put in my earrings or do up buttons - and my toes are too tender to wear my boots. I hobble slowly, like a little old lady. Small things, I agree, when compared to what else I might be dealing with, but discouraging and also upsetting this week. I'm not a good 'sick person'. Last evening and today I am finally feeling more energetic and less sore and my taste buds are coming back to normal - so I am happier and feeling more positive.

So - I had to choose again to have faith in the promises I feel God gave me at the beginning of all of this, that I would survive due to His care and the care of others, and look away from the pit at my feet to the light at the end of this journey - and practice saying again, "Thy will be done in my life/on earth, as it is in Heaven." It took a couple of days to get there, which is why I couldn't write earlier. But here I stand - thanks again for your prayers.

*"Yea, though I walk through the valley of the shadow of death, I will fear **no** evil, for Thou are with me; thy rod and thy staff they comfort me. " Psalm 23.4*

Radiation treatments continued through January and February into March. In this part of southwestern Ontario, this is when we get real winter, and the stretch of the 401 Highway between Chatham and Windsor can be treacherous. It has been nicknamed in spots "carnage alley" because of some fiery multiple vehicle collisions in bad weather with much loss of life. The highway sits a couple of feet higher than the surrounding farmland, and in freezing temperatures, the light blowing snow drifts across the road with the wind, and gets polished up like glass. The least intemperate move – over braking or over steering, a little too much speed or a gust of wind, can send even the best of drivers into difficult positions. The car that I had purchased in May of 2008, on which I had splurged for the latest technology in anti-skid protection, anti-lock braking, stability control and other features, in anticipation of long road trips together, now was a gift to us. I have considerable experience – about 45 to 50 years of driving in winter conditions in various locations in Canada, and with confidence in my vehicle I had little difficulty in navigating the winter roads.

Yet Helen was so appreciative of every trip, and as we backed into the garage at the end of a homeward leg, she would hug me and kiss me in the car as I turned off the engine, and thank me for driving her. Thank me? Why wouldn't I drive her? This was my fight as well as hers, but she never once took it for granted. I believe this is one of the things that kept our marriage healthy. One time at the dinner table, with just the two of us in our own home, I offered a bowl of food to her to see if she wanted an additional helping. She looked at me and said "You are so considerate. Thank you. You are always looking out for me and thinking of my good." I had to confess that I wanted to know if she wanted any more of whatever vegetable was in the dish, as little remained, or whether I could finish it off. Yet the act of asking her first, as insignificant as that might seem, she noted and thanked me for it. St. Paul's advice to husbands to "love your wives as you love your own bodies" is applicable in every nuance of marriage, not just the big decisions.

Sunday, January 18, 2009

It's been another very quiet week and I am reading, reading, reading - no idea how many books I have gone through since the beginning of this month! Lots of time on the couch - still not a lot of energy. However, I passed the 2-week mark on Friday from my last chemo and did not have to have more chemicals put in my body, so perhaps there will be an improvement this week.

Thursday, Jan. 15, I was supposed to have a treatment of the trial drug, Avastin, that would switch me over to a 3-week cycle. However, my blood pressure numbers for several days that week were too high and it was postponed to Jan.22. My b.p. meds have been doubled since Dec. 24 but the Avastin restricts the development of new blood vessels (would starve a newly-developing tumour) and must have some constrictive action on blood vessels too. I saw my doctor and came away with an additional b.p. med.! I am keeping track again and have to relay my numbers to Windsor on Wed. and that will determine if I get the treatment on Thursday or not.

Tomorrow, we start our daily trips to Windsor for my radiation course of treatments. These will continue every weekday until March 2. This is quite different from the chemo - just 15 min. It's more like a daily x-ray. I should have a couple of weeks of continued recovery time from the chemo while I start but then I have been told to expect to be the most tired the two weeks after I finish in March. Fortunately by then, there will be more sunshine and daylight and winter will be more or less over.

Thank you, again, to those of you who have been praying for David and I after my last post. We have regained our equilibrium and are doing

OK. I had to realize again that the doctor (radiologist) has to advise you of all possible outcomes of the new treatment you are beginning, no matter how small the chance is that it might happen to you. At my oncologist appointment on Thursday, I talked about my reactions and both the nurse and the doctor spoke about the way people feel when they finish chemo - no specific action left to be taken 'against the foe' - apparently I am right on track to be anxious, especially as a 'goal-oriented person'. But my doctor said, "You have done everything you were supposed to do - you have finished the course - it is gone." So - I was encouraged, and enlightened.

To those of you who do not live in this area - we are having a 'real winter' this year - received 20cm./8" MORE snow on Saturday and could not leave our house until our faithful farmer neighbour ploughed out our laneway. This makes the 5th time this season that he has had to do this - before Christmas, it was 3 times in one week. Those of you who live farther north may laugh at that 'little bit of snow' but it is a lot for us ! Everything is well blanketed with snow and on a sunny day it is quite pretty.

And, lastly, in another week, my hair should start growing back in !!! I have a good crop of stubble but it should start to grow seriously 3 weeks after the last chemo, which was Jan. 2.

Post a Comment On: <u>Helen's Journal</u>

Amanda said...

I'm glad things are once again looking up; don't worry too much about the hair growing back, you're beautiful with or without it.

I hope that you soon are back into your regular routine or skiing downhill in a beautiful place. Prayers like always,

Amanda

Sunday, February 1, 2009

First of all, I was able to have my Avastin treatment Jan. 22, so I am now on track to have this every 3 weeks until September...unless my blood pressure numbers get too high again, I guess. Everything went as it was supposed to and there was no problem with my port, as I have had before. Takes about 45 min. to 1 hr.

This is the longest I have gone without updating the blog - 2 weeks today! That will perhaps give you some idea of my fatigue level. However, I'll bring you up to date today.

Secondly, I have now had 9 radiation treatments in the last 2 weeks (the first day was a check film to make sure all alignments were correct.) There doesn't seem to be a lot to them - I just lie there on the gurney while the machine moves around me; I get 4 'shots' - front and back for lymph glands above my collar bone and also for my chest wall. The only way I know that anything is happening is the noise from the machine when it's radiating me - sounds like a little bagpipe drone. No pain, no heat - no sensation at all. It takes about 15 min. for the whole treatment but there's only about 1 min. 30 seconds combined of radiation. The rest is positioning, aligning and so on. Add to that 70 min. driving each way, plus a stop usually for lunch. Doesn't sound too bad but as the week goes along, I find myself getting more and more tired. I usually have to lie down for a while when we get home and am heading for bed around 9:00 p.m. most nights. My skin is fine so far - no sign of reddening anywhere from the radiation. I use lotion on the area most nights and so far, so good. Compared to the chemo treatments, there doesn't seem to be much actually happening to my body but the fatigue I am experiencing tells me otherwise.

So - 2 weeks done, 4 weeks plus a day to go. David drives me faithfully almost every day. He had to be in Toronto this past week and my sister was able to drive me Thursday and Friday. It was good to have some time with her. The weather has been co-operative for the most part; this past Wed. was not good but David has lots of experience in bad weather and we were fine. It continues to snow and we have had the laneway ploughed out another 3 times - brings us up to a total of 8.

Thank you again for your ongoing prayers as well as your cards. I appreciate them so much.

Here's the verse that was in my little devotional book last Wed. - "Daughter, thy faith hath made thee whole; go in peace, and be whole of thy plague. " Mark 5:34. I found it very comforting.

Sunday, February 8, 2009

Well, I have better news for you this week. Everything has gone according to schedule and I am also less tired than I have been for the last two weeks...actually feeling almost normal again. I saw my oncologist Monday and in the course of check-up questions realized that several things had improved without me noticing - my mouth lining is not bothering me any more, the tingling in my fingers only remains in my index fingers and thumbs and my big toes are not as sensitive - shoes don't hurt as much. So - gradual improvements and recovery from that last type of chemo. I still have to finish growing out my 'chemo nails' - we're about halfway on that. My blood pressure numbers weren't too good, though, so I was sent back to my family doctor, who is trying me on another medication which seems to be working already. Another improvement ! So, all in all, the news this week has been positive.

I am about the halfway point in my radiation treatments - Friday was #14 out of 29. No skin problems so far either. David will have to go out of town again this week so my daughter will come to drive me Thursday and Friday; it will be very good to see her again and will give her a chance to see where I have been going all these months.

The weather is changing again; temperatures have risen above freezing since Friday and there has been a lot of snow melt. Where we had drifts and snow piles higher than the cars in some areas we now have green patches showing through; we may lose all the snow if it continues and may have another danger of flooding, depending on how quickly it goes. It's been great to have the sunny days, though!

Thank you again for your cards and prayers - I'm so thankful for my good week.

Monday, February 16, 2009

I am happy to be able to report another good week. I continue to feel less tired and able to function more normally. I had all my scheduled radiation treatments and was able to have my Avastin treatment on Thursday as well. Blood pressure continues to be an issue with that but I just made it 'under the wire'. I am starting to have redness of skin in the chest area - you could practically put a ruler on it as the edges are quite clearly defined - but that is not only expected but desired, according to the radiation technicians. The tumour was quite close to my chest wall and they want to 'dose' the skin as well as the muscles in that area. I have been given hydrocortisone cream for the redness and it is helping.

David had to be in Toronto Thursday and Friday of the week, so my daughter came and drove me to Windsor for my appointments those days. It was great to have time with her and we got in a little 'shopping time' after I was finished at the Cancer Centre. I have been so thankful for the support and encouragement of my family during this time. David was back in time to treat us to a most enjoyable dinner out for Valentine's

Day, also much appreciated, complete with flowers.

I would ask for your prayers this week for my sister, though. She mis-stepped on her way to her bedroom Saturday night in the dark and fell down the entire staircase at her home, hitting a bench at the bottom of it as well. She had to be taken by ambulance to the hospital and has suffered broken ribs on both sides, a broken left wrist, dislocated left shoulder and many bumps and bruises. She was carrying a mug of hot milk; the mug struck the wall [broke] and cut her throat as well as her forehead and she has stitches in both locations. I have spoken to her several times by phone (she lives in Ottawa) and she seems better today but I am not able to go to see her because of my treatment schedule and that is hard. This will be a lot for her from which to recover; we don't bounce back quite a quickly as we get older.

I have received Valentines and Valentine gifts this week ! Thank you for remembering me still and for your kindness. Thank you also, of course, for your prayers. I never know who all is praying for me and it is comforting and touching to be out somewhere, meet someone I haven't seen for a while and have the conversation close with - "Oh - and I pray for you daily." It's really very humbling but I appreciate it so much and feel that it is one of the main reasons why I have been able to deal with this illness as well as I have.

May God be with you this week and may you be conscious of His presence with y

The fall that Helen's sister Carol in Ottawa had, troubled Helen greatly. In all the time I have known Helen, she has been an outgoing, caring person, quick to give comfort and encouragement, whether to her children, members of her family, teaching colleagues, or strangers. She always wished for a "magic wand" that could cure all ills, kiss all bumps and bruises and take away all pain. Our children in their younger years thought Helen should have some kind of Wonder Woman cape, as she flew from one crisis to another, bringing an end to tears, a hug and comfort. She was incredibly frustrated with guidelines for teachers in this modern age. Years ago, when she first started teaching a youngster, female or male, who had a tumble or bump and needing consoling would get a big hug from Mrs. Goldsmith or Madame Goldsmith. In her later years of teaching, because of unfortunate incidents of abuse of children of both sexes, it was hands off. She was not to touch a child for fear that parents would distort that touch into something ugly, and cause problems. I know on many occasions that Helen simply let her mothering instincts take over, and ignored the rules and would give a comforting hug or cuddle to a whimpering 6 or 7 year old child, because she simply felt that was the right thing to do.

With Carol injured in the Ottawa hospital, Helen was deeply torn. She needed to continue her own treatment schedule in Windsor, but she needed to be with her sister. Carol lives by herself, although she does have a male boarder in her house. Fortunately that boarder was able to call 911 after Carol's fall, but was unable to do things for her that a sister could. In fact for the first couple of days after Carol's fall, he was grilled by Ottawa police, who seemed convinced that he had caused Carol's injuries.

There is a theme throughout Helen's blog. Her concern for other people. In spite of all that she was enduring, her concern was for her sister, and for me. Not that her sister's injuries were in any way trivial; they were extremely serious, as were my bouts of vertigo and falls. But it seemed that Helen put all concern for herself on the back burner, when someone needed her care, and focused all of her attention on her role as caregiver.

Tuesday, February 24, 2009

Coming down to the wire, friends ! Today will be my last 'main' radiation treatment; then 4 "booster' treatments on a smaller area (same location). I'll be done radiation completely next Monday, March 2. There will be a follow-up appointment with my radiation doctor and then that will be it. This Thursday, I also go to a lymphodema clinic to learn about future care of the arm on the surgery side - left, in my case. Because of the number of lymph nodes that were removed, I can never use that arm for blood pressure readings or blood sampling again - nothing that will restrict fluid flow. Plus, there are some other restrictions and care, all to avoid swelling in that arm. Something new to learn every day !

I have come through the radiation treatments quite well - I have a burn area 8" x 6" on my chest wall - surgery site - but no blistering or cracking, as was mentioned in the initial warnings. I have hydrocortisone cream to apply twice daily and that keeps me comfortable. The burn is red, like a sunburn, but doesn't have that burning sensation, fortunately - just a tightness in certain spots. It will recover and heal, of course. And - I now have eyebrow 'stubble', where my eyebrows are starting to re-grow! Eyelashes are showing up, too, and my 'halo' continues to show up in the light more and more. I've learned this winter that you really do lose a lot of body heat from your head!

My dear sister is still in hospital in Ottawa, recovering from her dreadful fall. She will move to a short-term rehabilitation centre at another hospital later this week, since she would not be able to manage at home yet. Most of her injuries are on the left side - broken wrist, dislocated shoulder, possible concussion, six broken ribs, a cut from left eyebrow to hairline, another cut below her left ear on her throat from the mug, needing 13 stitches, plus lots of bruising -and she will need time before she can do stairs and lots of other things. Please remember her in your prayers.

Thank you again for your prayers for me during this time of illness. There's a big light at the end of the tunnel ! I'll still be getting the trial drug, Avastin, every three weeks until the end of September, but after March 2, my life should be more or less back to normal.

May God's presence be known to you this week.

Post a Comment On: Helen's Journal

Sharon said...

Helen, I am so excited that your treatments are almost over. My prayers include you so

very often. You are a precious friend and I long to see you completely well.
It would be wonderful to see the two of you. We are well except for Tom's miserable cold. But he will recover.
Love you loads,
Sharon

Amanda said...

Well, prayers for three it is!
May god bless not only you and your journey of safe and active living, but bless the hearts of your husband and your sister. If anything like yourself, they deserve the encouragement!
Have a great, happy, and SAFE week.
yours sincerely
Amanda

Tuesday, March 3, 2009

Greetings ! Yes, I finished my radiation treatments yesterday ! It seems rather unreal and will take a few days to sink in, I guess. I have an Avastin treatment on Thursday, so I won't be away from Windsor too long. However, after that, I think things will feel like they have changed, since I will only have to go back every 3 weeks now until September. I am tired, as I was advised I would be, and my radiation burn area is sore in a couple of spots, but that's all. I have cream to apply and I do! So it is now just a question of healing and recovering from all the treatments that I have had over the last 6 months.

Today brought a new health surprise for David. He had been noticing a dark spot in his right eye for several days, rather like an eclipse taking over part of his vision. It didn't hurt although it was tricky to read; still went to Toronto for his meeting on Friday and Saturday.

(Our youngest son and his fiancée had come to drive me to Windsor.) Today we went to our optometrist and were told that he has a 25% detachment of the retina - quite a shock. He is scheduled for surgery at the Ivey Institute at Victoria Hospital in London tomorrow. We have to be there for 8:00 a.m. so it will be an early start ! As far as we know, he will be coming home the same day. We would appreciate your prayers for this situation.

My sister is still in hospital in Ottawa after her fall. She had surgery last Friday to correct her shoulder position and her wrist, since the doctors were not pleased with the way they were healing. This was unexpected and painful. Yesterday, she was moved to a rehab unit at another hospital where she will be for 5 - 7 days while she is helped to learn techniques for dressing, showering and getting up out of a normal (flat) bed. Her left arm is in a sling to support her shoulder and her wrist is in a partial cast, so she has little use from it.

So there you have it. You never know what a day will bring ! Thanks again for your prayers.

__Tuesday, March 10, 2009__

Another interesting week! We made it to London in good time last Wednesday - David drove there - and had several eye examinations at the Ivey Institute on the south side of London. It was determined that surgery was needed and we were sent across town to St. Joseph's Hospital on the north side, where the ophthalmology surgery is done. After going through the regular admitting routines, we waited for a time slot and were fortunate to be called around 4:15 p.m. - could have been between 7 - midnight! The actual surgery took about 45 min. and by 5:45 I was back with David and we were being told we could go home. We were able to leave around 6:30 and had supper in London before driving home. [Helen drove!] What a day ! He had to sleep face down that night, because of the gas bubble in his eye holding the retina against the back of his eye. We were asked to return Thursday afternoon for a check-up, so I called Windsor and put my Avastin treatment over to Friday.

Good sleep for both of us that night and off to London again for the check-up. When the shield came off David's eye, it was a sight to behold - purple, swollen and the eyeball itself a blood red. Also, he could not see anything out of it, which was rather scary. However, it has improved daily and his vision is returning little by little. We return to London Tuesday March 24 for another check up and it will be interesting to see how much it has improved by then.

I drove myself to Windsor on Friday for my Avastin treatment, which went very well - a non-event. My blood pressure was exceptionally good, my port wasn't clogged - even had a nap while it was going in. If I had not been admitted to this clinical trial, I would have finished going to Windsor at the end of my radiation. As it is, I will see my oncologist every 3 weeks until Sept. and then every 3 months for 2 years and then every 6 months for the next 2 years, so I will be well supervised. Since this type of cancer has a high rate of return in the first three years, that is especially good. Once I pass that three-year point, I will be considered 'out of the woods'.

My sister is continuing to do well at the rehab and will probably be going home this coming Friday. That will be a month from the time of her fall. She is looking forward to getting out of the hospital but also realizing that this will present new challenges to her. She won't be driving for a while, so has to make arrangements with the ParaTranspo service and a few other things like that. I am planning to take the train to Ottawa next week and spend some time with her.

Yesterday, we were saddened by the news of the death of our youngest son's fiancée's mother. She had surgery Dec. 11 for removal of her gall bladder; at that time multiple tumours were discovered in her digestive system and it was not possible to remove all of them. We had hoped for a longer time for her, but it was not to be. We plan to attend the funeral this weekend.

So - we go from day to day. Robins have returned, daffodils are poking up, spring is on its way. Thank you again for your prayers and for your thoughtfulness in sending cards. A special thank you to a good neighbour who magically brings chili on nights when I haven't got the energy to cook. May all your kindnesses come back to you !

Sunday, March 15, 2009

We've just returned from a weekend in Kitchener- Waterloo where we attended the funeral of our youngest son's fiancée's mother. It was actually a very encouraging experience - a very strong family, strong in their love and support for each other and strong in their faith that their wife and mother is safe in Heaven's keeping.

Tomorrow, I take the train (the really early one!) to Ottawa to spend the week with my sister. I am looking forward to seeing her and being able to help her as she adjusts back to regular living. David is staying here and looking forward to a quiet week - not having to drive anyone anywhere !!

There's not much else to report - I'll bring news from Ottawa and elsewhere when I get back after March Break. Thanks again for your prayers for all of us.

Monday, April 6, 2009

Greetings! Well, a lot more time has gone by since I last wrote than I expected. The principal reason for that is my extended stay in Ottawa with my sister. I travelled there by train Monday,

March 16 and was only there a couple of days when I realized that I needed to stay longer than I had planned. Broken ribs cannot be stabilized with bandaging or casts and almost every time she changed position, something shifted and hurt. Add to that a left shoulder needing a sling and a left wrist in a support/half cast and you are down to one working arm. So I was able to be chauffeur, sometime cook and general handy person for her for 2 weeks. I could have stayed longer, but I had my own medical appointments to keep back here. She is improving but it will still be several weeks before she has the use of her left arm and those ribs heal.

We were able to get in some visits with cousins and I still have a good friend from high school that I was also able to see, so we had some fun times, too.

I returned home by train Sunday, March 29 and had my last (I think) MUGA scan for my heart Monday and my delayed Avastin treat-

ment in Windsor on Tuesday. Neither of these causes me any physical distress and I am now just generally recovering from the whole treatment procedure. I find that I do not need my afternoon rests as much - just every couple of days now, depending on what else I am doing, instead of every day. Also, my hair has grown back in enough that I have stopped wearing my wig and go out 'au naturel' now. It's quite grey/silvery and still quite short, so I look very different from what people are used to but it is a relief to be bare-headed again without the constriction of the wig. I practiced in Ottawa to get used to it and am now letting the 'home folks' recognize the new me.

It is David who is keeping us from getting bored these days - he has had to have a second eye surgery for his detaching retina. He had a follow-up appointment Tuesday, March 24 for the first surgery - the second week that I was in Ottawa. Fortunately, our daughter was able to go with him to that appointment and when the doctor decided that a second surgery was necessary, she was able to stay and go with her dad to that, too. We certainly appreciated her help, both with her dad and for making it possible for me to stay in Ottawa with my sister. His second surgery was Friday, March 27 and he is still having some discomfort and other issues with it. After my Avastin treatment last Tuesday, I drove with him to Sarnia for his Board of Education meeting, so that I could drive home and those of you who know him will realize what a concession that is! Between the darkness and the forecasted rain, he did not feel that he could see well enough to drive home alone. He has a follow-up appointment next week and we will see what comes from that.

So - there you have it ! We are keeping on keeping on ! Thank you so much for your prayers and your ongoing interest and concern. We certainly appreciate them. I hope you have a blessed Easter, however you celebrate it and have time to remember and be thankful for the tremendous gift God gave through Christ's death and resurrection. Without it, we would have no reason to pray or to hope; I would have had no one to turn to these last few months for strength or hope as I faced this disease. But because of it and because I have chosen to place my trust in Him, I have been able to face it in confidence that my life is safe in His care and with faith that He is guiding and protecting me through this time. As the scriptures say, "Whoever will, may come" - it is a gift open to any who will choose it.

Friday, April 17, 2009

As you see, time between posts is extending and for a very good reason. There is less and less to report on - we are all getting better!

I am feeling better and stronger all the time, although I am not back to what I was before all this started. I'm now trying to sort out what is age-related fatigue and what is still recovery from medical treatments. Hard to know ! I was outside working for an hour or so yesterday in the sun and then sat for a while on the front porch in my favourite spot - more sun! Felt wonderful! Then I was in bed by 8:30...slept 12 hours. So - hard to tell. I'm desperately out of shape, one way or another and that will be my main project this spring and summer.

David had a follow-up visit to his eye surgeon this week and all is going well there, too. He has stitches in his eye which will dissolve but are still irritating. It will be 6 - 9 months before his vision has stabilized completely although he can see better all the time.

My sister continues to improve as well although it is also a slow process for her. The pins are out of her wrist, stitches for that are removed, sling is not needed all the time, and physiotherapy is helping. Those broken ribs are still painful though and she still is using a cane.

She gets to her office about three days a week and continues to work from home at other times as she has been doing right along. Ottawa has a great ParaTranspo service and this is her transportation most of the time.

So - we see on-going improvements and are getting back into life. It's so good to feel healthy again ! Thank you for your on-going prayers.

Final Post - Thursday, May 7, 2009

Why final ?? Because there's so little to report ! You can see that the time between posts has gotten longer and longer. That shows that I am better and better, doing more and more things that are part of normal life. I went to the USA with a group of girlfriends the last weekend in April to go shopping - had a great time ! David and I went to Toronto last weekend to attend a surprise birthday party for a dear friend of many years. We're heading out of town for Mother's Day and later this month, flying to

Texas to spend time with family there and help our granddaughter celebrate her first birthday. I have been digging over flower beds and starting a new one, cutting the grass, and other usual household chores. So you can see that my energy level is much improved, along with my general health. I feel almost back to normal and am so thankful to be there. Thank you all again so much for your prayers and love and support as I passed through this experience. It was humbling but such a comfort to know that so many took me 'under their wing' and held me up in prayer. It gave me courage.

The other big lesson I learned (re-learned?) through this is that God is present and active in our everyday lives; we have only to ask. I returned often to the promises I felt I had been given at the start of this and took strength and courage from them to keep on going. I can see so many ways that He provided, and continues to provide opportunities to be cared for and to get through this. Thanks be to God !

David continues to see improvement in his eye, although it is slower than he would wish. It tires as the day goes along and he often has a headache by the end of the day. He has a follow-up appointment early in June, so he is still under the doctor's observation and care.

My sister was able to start driving herself last week and is enjoying the freedom that has been restored to her. That also means that she is at work longer, because there is no reason that she has to leave. She started working 5 days this week and is planning to attend a major annual conference for her profession in Calgary at the end of this month. So she is better, but still sore and still tires from the pain of the ribs and shoulder. It's a long process and she hasn't really been 'off work' to recover; the computer and the phone have always been there.

Once again, I thank you so much for your interest, love, support and prayers. It was pretty scary there for a while but it looks like we're back in the sunshine and on the open road again. God is able !

(I plan to write again in September when I come off the trial drug and add any news that will result from that, but not until then unless there is other news.)

Post a Comment On: <u>Helen's Journal</u>
Candy said...

Hi Helen,

I am so glad that everything has worked out so well for you. I have been praying for you everyday. Enjoy the children and your garden.

Much love,
Candy

Chapter Six

It's Back

September and the months following merged into a blur. Life was going well; Helen was feeling great. My eye was still giving me problems, but I was learning to live with compromised vision in one eye. In the process of the retina detaching twice, and the two surgeries to repair it, a tiny cyst had formed directly in the centre of my retina. The result was a very tiny blind spot in the centre of my vision. The sight had returned to the rest of the eye, but when I looked directly at something, straight lines became distorted and seemed to be pulled into some kind of black hole in the middle of my vision. People's heads disappeared as I was talking with them. Reading became diffi

I was still legally able to drive, as hundreds of people across the country drive with sight in only one eye. On one trip up to Kitchener to see our daughter, youngest son and chosen daughter to be, I tried to encourage Helen by describing what I could see. While in the left lane of a four-lane highway, I closed my left (good) eye and described to Helen what I saw. I told her I could see the yellow line along the left edge of the pavement, the white, broken centre line, and the white line at the far right edge of the pavement. "What do you see in the right lane," she asked. "Nothing" I replied. That probably was not a reassuring answer, because there was a semi-truck in the right lane, that I knew was there, and was about to pass, but honestly could not see with only my damaged eye. After a solemn promise to only drive with both eyes open, we proceeded.

My vision problem also, at least temporarily, ended another chapter in my life. I love to read. I learned to read at a very early age, at home, before starting kindergarten. Helen and I read to all of our children, nightly, and all four of them were reading at an advanced level before starting school. I read to my grandchildren at every opportunity, and even created a poster using a photo taken by my daughter of my grandson Clay stretched out on my chest, as I lay on a couch reading a book to him. The poster said "Literacy begins at home" and I distributed 450 copies of it to schools, libraries, retail store windows, bank and grocery store bulletin boards. I even learned there was one on the wall of the office of the Ontario Minister of Education who had seen it and requested one. As a parent, as the spouse of an elementary teacher, and as an elected public school board trustee, I was convinced that if a child did not learn to read well, by the end of the third grade, that that child was going to be handicapped in his or her academic career and throughout the rest of that person's life. So, I began to conduct reading camps at some elementary schools, and read to children from kindergarten through grade four. I had a variety of motivations to do this. First was my belief that a solid ability to read was the foundation for life. Secondly, I wanted children, especially the boys, to see a male person who loved books and loved to read. Thirdly, many of these children came from dysfunctional homes, perhaps without a father, or with a father who wanted to sit on the couch and watch TV. I wanted to be a positive male image to them. Finally, it was just plain fun. My two grandchildren were 1500 miles away in Texas, and other people's children became my surrogate grandchildren for a couple of hours in a week. Sadly, however, because of the damaged retina, I had to give up reading in elementary schools.

God truly works in mysterious ways, and we saw evidence of this throughout Helen's journey. In mid-September, Helen had a persistent pain in her side. Having already had both her gall bladder and appendix removed, we were perplexed as to what could be the cause. She contacted her doctor in Windsor, and discussed this pain, and the doctor knowing that breast cancer spreads to four main areas – lung, liver, bones and brain – scheduled a CT scan for Helen. The results showed no sign of any cause of pain in her abdomen, but did show some scatted, tiny white spots on her lungs. The pain in her side disappeared shortly after the scan and never returned. However, the pain had precipitated the CT scan and Helen was back on everyone's radar. A follow-up CT scan was scheduled for November 23rd, and an appointment scheduled with the oncologist for January 12th, 2010.

In October, our second granddaughter, Emmy arrived in Texas, eight weeks prior to her expected birth date. This captivated our time and attention, with daily bulletins from the NICU in an Austin hospital. God again provided for our family, and our Texas children live only blocks from one of the most advanced hospitals in the United States, focused especially on "preemies." Thanks to modern technology Steve kept us up to date with images shot on his BlackBerry, immediately sent to us by e-mail. Hundreds of family members and friends prayed daily for little Emmy. Not content with the electronic images, Helen had to make a trip down to Austin, to hold this tiny bundle to her breast and coo and sing to her.

November 23rd, Helen had the CT scan as planned. We then proceeded to make plans for Christmas in Texas. We were going to rent a house through Steve's company, an online portal through which people all over the world who want to rent out their homes to guests, can be connected to people who wanted short term rentals. Helen found a lovely home with five bedrooms, three baths, a huge dinning room and a cozy family room, near our Texas children, but far enough away not to be underfoot. Emmy was discharged from hospital just prior to Christmas, and baby and mother needed quiet and rest. However, with the huge dining room at the rental house, Christmas dinner could be held there, and allow Steve and Kristen's family to come and go as they needed.

December 9th, the telephone rang, telling us that we had an unexpected appointment with Helen's oncologist in Windsor on December 14th. As we made the trip to Windsor, in light of the urgency of the appointment, we speculated that we were going to receive bad news, but we were still not prepared for the news that the doctor had to deliver. The cancer was back. It was in both lungs. It was now stage IV. It was terminal. After many hugs and tears, we made our way back to Chatham. During the trip we agreed to put a brave face on this news, to keep it to ourselves, not to share it with the children or other family members, and not to spoil Christmas. We would go ahead with our Austin trip as planned, and then in January face up to whatever had to be confronted.

Long-promised Update Jan.6, 2010

Greetings to all !

I had said in my last entry that I would return in September, when I finished my Avastin treatments, to let you know how things were going. Well, things were going so well in September, October and November that I just didn't get back to it. In October, we became grandparents again, as our son and daughter-in-law in Texas became proud parents of their second daughter. However, she arrived 8 weeks early and was the

Big News for several weeks. She is now doing very well. I was able to spend a week there in November and enjoyed myself immensely. So those months were full and happy and I was feeling great. Family plans for Christmas were to rent a house in Austin and spend two weeks there, with various children coming and going as they were able. We were able to get a 5-bedroom, 3,000 sq. ft. place through my son's business and it was looking good.

However, cancer never sleeps, you know and there was other stuff happening. I think I will give you a time-line here, so that you can see how events unfolded.

Sept. 16 – finished Avastin treatments

Sept. 24 (or so) – had an unscheduled CT scan, chest and abdomen, because of a persistent ache in my right side. (Breast cancer can spread to lungs, liver, brain and bones – still treated as breast cancer). Abdomen was clear, but chest showed particulates in lungs; follow-up CT scan booked for Nov. 23

Oct. 1 – went to Seattle to see son and fiancée for a week's visit

Oct. 14 – 4-week check-up after finishing Avastin; next check-up booked for Jan. 12

Oct. 20 – new granddaughter, Emmy, arrives, 8 weeks early

* Somewhere in here I joined the Active Lifestyle Centre and started taking line-dancing lessons

Nov. 14 – flew to Austin for 'grandma week'

Nov. 23 – follow-up CT scan (Nov. 25 – gastroscopy for unhappy tummy)

Dec. 9 – call from my oncologist to book unscheduled visit Dec. 14 – not a good sign

- Texas baby comes home after 50 days in the NICU

Dec. 14 – devastating visit – bad news – cancer has spread to both lungs – I have to have more chemo and soon – would have me in right away if I wasn't going to Texas – will start Jan. 4. This was one of the most surreal experiences of my life – I literally thought she had the wrong person for a minute, but the look on her face told me otherwise. We went home in shock – how could this possibly be true? Very bad night – made worse for my children and extended family because I confused the terms 'non-curable' and 'palliative' – thought they were the same, but my sister corrected me. 'Non-curable' = chronic, with lots of treatment options (which is where I am!) but 'palliative' = nothing more can be done. I had to really hang on tight to God.

Dec. 15 – gastroscopy result = chronic gastritis = new meds = better

Dec. 16 – Christmas Assembly at my former school – I had the wonderful experience of leading the Christmas carols at the end – a real pick-me-up. However, pretty hard not to say something to dear friends there, but we had decided to let it rest until after Christmas and deal with it then. Some of them could 'read' me though and knew something was wrong. My news is also on the church prayer chain and will be in the bulletin on Sunday, so the word will get out. I want to be the one to let people know in quite a few cases – timing, timing !

Dec. 17 – Annual Christmas dinner with my teaching buds -- a group that has been together 12+ years – after consultation, I decided to send them an e-mail Wed. night so that they knew but I didn't have to tell them face-to-face. We had a few hugs and tears and then had a wonderful evening together, as always.

Dec. 18 – here's where it gets interesting ! My Texas son called to ask if I would consider seeing doctors there during our holiday. I agreed as long as it didn't create any conflict with my wonderful oncologist here. We agreed that he would try to get an appointment with a nutrition PhD who specializes in treating cancer patients. When he called, he was told it would probably be a 6-week wait, and for a phone consultation, but to leave his name in case of a cancellation. 2 hours later, we had an office appointment Tuesday morning at 9:30 – we were arriving Monday night. (I found out later that my daughter-in-law's sister had an appointment Wed. which she would have given me if nothing else worked out.) So – the first amazing thing was set up.

Dec. 19 – lovely dinner with a school friend who 'read' me Dec. 16- told the whole story and then had a nice evening together.

Dec. 20, 21 – Christmas Sunday – first public prayer for my health again – tears – so thankful for my church family. Also travel to Detroit that night and then flight to Austin Monday. Rental house is terrific ! Five of us there by that night – big reunion with Texas crew. First visit for everyone except me with new baby.

Dec. 22 – appointment with nutrition PhD. This was an amazing experience in so many ways. I brought my medical information with me to the appointment, including a page on my Canadian oncologist, for background info. On the page facing that, I had a copy of a page of scripture, 2 Samuel 22: 1 – 7, 17 – 22, that I had typed out for another friend who had dealt with cancer 7 –8 years ago – seemed timely for me now. As I put the binder up on the Dr.'s desk, he spotted the scripture and read it and then said to me – "OK – from now on, whenever you see your doctors, I want you to pray the prayer of Jeremiah 33:3 for them." That established an immediate spiritual connection for me – I felt so clearly that God had brought me to this man and that I was in the right place. He went on to give me two things: A list of nutritional guidelines to follow as I battle this disease and a referral to the Mary Crowley Cancer Research Center in Dallas. I could hardly believe my ears – what was a little Canuck doing at a research center in Dallas ?? My daughter and my Texas son were with me and took copious notes at this appointment.

Dec. 24 – we have an appointment in Dallas Dec. 30 ! God at work again – through the people that He has made available to me, including my Texas son who wants this to happen, big time.

Dec. 26 – the one day that we are all together at the rental house – able to have a huge Christmas dinner for 12 and a wonderful time. My sister didn't make it 'til midnight, due to weather problems on the east coast, but we counted her and she had turkey before she went to bed !

Dec. 27, 29 – various family members leave, sadly – we've had a great time together.

Dec. 30 – 4 of us (David and I, my sister and our Texas son) drive to Dallas to my appointment – 453 mi. round-trip. We have an hour's consultation there and I am offered the chance to return for screening into another clinical trial for a phase 2 drug if my scheduled chemo here in Windsor does not prove effective against the cancer. There are another couple of options as well. We leave with a 21-page consent form for informational purposes ! Lots of technical reading ! I am amazed all over again at the doors that God is opening for me. Because it is a privately-funded hospital, and a clinical trial, there would be very few actual expenses for me, if I need to go this route. We went out to a steak restaurant for lunch to celebrate ! I had a buffalo filet – excellent – try it if you get the chance.

Jan. 2 – packed up and flew back to cold weather – but bringing a big load of hope as well! God is busy for me !

Jan. 4 – first chemo in Windsor (carbo-platinum, if you're interested). I also took my oncologist a packet of all the info I had received in Texas, plus a cover letter asking for time to talk about this. She's incredibly busy right now, so time will tell.

Jan. 6 – going to London today with David for his pre-op appointment for his cataract surgery next week, Jan. 13 – hoping that this will brighten up his vision considerably, as it has been quite discouraging for him.

So – there you are! Up to date again! I can't really tell you how much hope I came back with from Texas – such a confirmation that God is still in this with me and it helps so much to keep positive and focused on doing everything I can to battle this disease. I know that this will be a shock for some of you and please understand that if I saw you that week of Dec. 14 and didn't say anything, it was because I just couldn't then. And now that I can tell you all the wonderful things that happened in Texas, it is a much happier story, anyhow ! What if I hadn't had that CT scan back in September ? I wouldn't be seeing my oncologist until Jan. 12 !!!

Call me if you want – I can talk about it much better now. Thank you for your ongoing concern and prayers.

I'll keep my blog up to date now and the story unfolds.

Our intent to keep the news secret lasted until the first telephone call from Helen's sister Carol, to ask how the doctor's visit had gone. Our resolve completely evaporated, and over the course of a couple of weeks, we shared the news with family and friends. Prayer warriors kicked into high gear again. We never ceased to be amazed at all of the people praying daily for Helen. There was a prayer chain at our church in Chatham, but it did not end there. During my time in Ohio we had worshiped at Dublin Baptist Church and were members of an aptly named Sunday school class called the "Encouragers Class." While Helen did not live with me in Ohio, she drove down one weekend a month. I was very active in the music ministry of the church, so three Sundays a month, I was with the Dublin church choir, one of those Sundays with Helen in the congregation. I came to Chatham one Sunday a month so that we were together every other weekend. The Encouragers Class had its own prayer chain, and upheld her daily.

Our son Peter in Seattle was engaged to a young woman whose parents lived in Chicago. Jocelyn's mother talked to the prayer chain in her (Chicago) church and people there began to pray. Jocelyn's family had roots in Kentucky and an aunt and uncle who were part of a prayer ministry there took on the task of praying for Helen. One of my cousins in Chatham, a semi-retired hair dresser does hair styling for nuns in an Ursuline Motherhouse in the area. Beth mentioned her cousin's prayer need and the nuns committed to include Helen in their daily prayers. A waitress in a diner on the outskirts of Windsor, where we often stopped for a bite to eat on the way home from the hospital, knowing that there was a regional cancer centre in the city, and having us suddenly pop up out of nowhere and appear on a regular basis, was prompted to ask if one of us was having cancer treatment. We identified Helen as the patient, and the woman asked "Would you mind if I asked what your name is so I can give it to the prayer chain at my church?" People all over North America who we had never met prayed faithfully for us every day. With what little I knew about the various prayer chains and the numbers of their members, I estimated that on any given day, over 1000 people were praying for Helen by name.

God continued to open doors. Through Kristen's family Steve became aware of an oncologist in Austin, who was also a PhD in nutrition. Steve contacted this doctor to see if Helen could get a consult while we were in Texas for Christmas. The doctor's office regretfully told Steve that the earliest possible date was at least six weeks out, and it could only a telephone conversation. Committing this into God's hands, Helen and I jumped on a plane in Detroit and headed to Texas – land of warmth, sunshine, grandchildren! While we were in mid-air on the flight south, Steve got a telephone call from the doctor's office in Austin. He had a cancellation for the next day. Could we be in his office on the day after our arrival in Texas? Because of the changes in cabin pressure on the airplane, I was fighting considerable pain in my damaged eye, and opted to remain at the rental house. Steve, our daughter Amy and Helen went to the appointment. Helen came back supercharged, first to have learned that this doctor was a fellow believer, confirming for her that God's hand was at work in connecting her to him, and secondly because this oncologist was referring Helen to the Mary Crowley Cancer Research Center in Dallas.

On December 30th, we went to meet with the second doctor in Dallas. He described some of the experimental work they were doing. This was extreme cutting edge, including some patients where a vaccine was made from the patients cancer cells DNA, a vaccine which then was programmed to specifically attack cells with that DNA. We were delighted with the possibilities and came back to Canada with a stack of consent forms, a ton of literature to read, and a website address where we could look on-line at the research being done.

We came back to Canada, however, with some trepidation. While funding for research is provided to the cancer research center by a foundation established by a wealthy Texas woman – Mary Crowley, and by pharmaceutical companies, all scans, lab tests and other non-medication expenses, including air fares, hotel rooms and meals would have to be paid by us, and our Canadian Government health care plan would not cover these costs. Also high on our anxiety list was how to broach this subject with Helen's oncologist in Windsor. Would she view this as a lack of confidence on our part of her skills and knowledge? Would she be offended and want to drop Helen as a patient if Helen was not satisfied with what she was doing? How could we afford all of these expensive tests? I was prepared to pay whatever it took, but as two retirees on a fixed income, the money pit was not bottomless. All of our fears were groundless. Our meeting with Dr. Hamm on January 4th was very encouraging. She determined that the Dallas team, were just one more tool in her arsenal, and now knowing that we were prepared to travel outside of Canada for treatment, described to us clinical trials going on in Maryland and other locations across the USA. She developed a plan to work with the Texas research center, by arranging as many as possible of the lab tests and scans to be done in Canada, where our government health plan would pay for them, and then sharing electronically the test results with the Dallas team. Rather than treating this as a competition to her, she seemed to view it as a learning experience to broaden her understanding of what was available "out there" in her determined fight against cancer.

Wednesday, January 20, 2010

A Prayer of Faith

This past fall, I was asked to compose a 'prayer of faith' as part of a study book on the Book of Hebrews for our church. It was due by Sept. 13. On that morning, (I had been thinking about it for several days but had nothing on paper), I wrote this on my daughter's computer in Kitchener and e-mailed it to the person in Chatham who had asked for it. I thought I was almost all done with my cancer treatments at that point - my last Avastin dose was to be Sept.

16. However, time has proved otherwise and this prayer has been a comfort and a reminder. So often, in this cancer experience, God has provided for me before I knew what I needed. I publish it here in hopes that it may also be a help to someone else.

A Prayer of Faith

O God !
Have mercy, I pray !
Deliver me from the onslaught of these fears -
These dark imaginings,
These dreadful possibilities that are only that -
Possibilities - NOT facts.
They roll over me like the waves of the sea,
And fill me with despair.
Help me to realize that the voice that whispers
them in my mind
Is neither mine - nor yours.
Help me instead to turn my thoughts to You -
To remember Your precious promises

Given so often and so clearly in Your Word -
To comfort and sustain,
To defend and protect,
To fight for those who put their trust in You.
Help me to go over them, Lord,
The ones You have given me,
Word by word,
Promise by promise,
Step by faltering step,
Until I reach Your peace -
Until I am enfolded by the Comforter -
Until I am safe in the light of Your love -
And I can truly speak the prayer
That never fails -
"Thy will be done."

Thank you, O Lord, my God,
For Your sustaining love and grace.
Amen.

Post a Comment On: Helen's Journal

Gail said...

Hi Helen:

I just decided to visit your page here to see if you had written anything since last spring. Was I surprised to hear this news. I felt better after reading your last piece though and continue to keep you in my prayers. You are such an inspiration to everyone with your positive words and I will use your prayer often I am sure. Talk to you soon. Love Gail

Wednesday, January 20, 2010

Results of This Morning's Visit to my Oncologist

My visit to my oncologist this a.m. has gone extremely well. She is very supportive of the Texas options and we have agreed on the following plan:

1) CT scan to be scheduled the week of Feb. 8, following second chemo Jan. 25

2) CT scan should be read by Feb. 12

3) Third chemo is scheduled for Feb. 16; this will be the decision day, as I will have an exam first. We will either proceed with the third chemo because it is working or stop because it is not and begin planning with Dallas to see when I could go there for screening to see if I qualify for their clinical trial.

She also told us about another group of trial drugs, called PARP-1 inhibitors. There is a clinical trial for that just starting in Bethesda, Maryland but since I have already started treatment with carboplatinum, I am not eligible for it. However, she said that more trials would be set up in the future and that I might be eligible for one of those. Now that she knows we will travel for treatment, she can again offer more options. If I don't need to go to Dallas this time, it may also be an option for future treatments, since you have to keep changing the 'attack drug' - cancer cells adapt very quickly apparently and become resistant, once they have been 'chemoed' with a drug.

So - lungs 'sound good' again, metastases are very small, detection was early, I feel great, God is good. We are quite relieved, and don't have to go back to Windsor until Monday !

David's eye is getting better by the day although it is still quite pink. His cataract surgery was Jan. 13, a week ago today. He also had the silicone oil removed from his eye and the combination of new lens and clearer fluid has resulted in much better vision. He is seeing improvement daily although that black space in the centre from the tiny cyst is still there. He can adapt by moving the centre of his vision around, to see what he is missing.

Thank you again for all the prayers offered on our behalf.

Chapter Seven

The Texas Trial

I have dedicated this book to our four children. At the outset of this chapter, I am going to digress slightly, to give you some family background, and help you to understand our children, in order that you can see the way that Helen invested in her kids, and how that investment was paid back to her during this most difficult journey.

In the six years of our marriage prior to the birth of our daughter Amy, Helen and I had many talks about the family that we hoped God would give to us. We decided we wanted five children.

We did not specify what gender we wanted these children to be, but we wanted at least one girl and one boy.

In addition to the number of children that we aspired to have, Helen wanted most of all to have a family of children who would truly love each other, support each other and return love to us. This was her reason to take 18 years out of her career to raise our children, to help achieve this goal. She succeeded. Amy arrived in May of 1973 and Steve followed very closely in September of 1974. Peter was born 30 months after Steve, in March of 1977. At this point, Helen re-calibrated her desire for five children. Peter was a difficult pregnancy, a very large baby and a difficult natural birth, and she decided she did not want to have any more children. In her caring attitude towards me, which she exhibited throughout our marriage, she suggested she have a tubal ligation. I offered to have a vasectomy, but her logic was that if something happened to her, and I remarried, she wanted me to be able to have future children with another wife, should I chose to do so.

Helen never quite got around to that tubal ligation. In July of 1978 she finally made an appointment with our doctor to schedule the surgery. In preparation she was given a routine pregnancy test. Surprise! Helen was six week pregnant. We were horrified when doctor and nurses assured us that this was not an issue and that the "problem" could be taken care of. Helen was aghast, and stated unequivocally that if God wanted her to have another child, another child it would be. In March of 1979, eight days before his closest brother's second birthday, Michael Andrew arrived to make our family complete. Years later, Helen and I reflected that without Michael, Peter would have had a somewhat lonely existence. Amy and Steve were so close in age, and did so much together, that they did not necessarily want their little brother tagging along. Peter, however, was growing so rapidly and looked so much older than his chronological age that he wanted to be part of everything Amy and Steve did. With his little brother, Mikey, Peter was content and he and Mike were the closest of friends.

As the children grew and matured, there was inevitable competition. All four of them were classified as gifted by the educational system, and provided a unique challenge and responsibility to Helen and I. She stepped up to the challenge and strove to make her children's upbringing a rich, happy, fun and loving environment. She more than achieved her goal for her family to be close and loving people. This became more evident as the children grew, completed secondary school and went on to university. All three boys attended the University of Waterloo in Ontario, sometimes referred to as "Canada's MIT." Amy attended the University of Guelph, which about a hundred years ago started out as an agricultural school and is now Canada's premier veterinary university, in addition to a wonderful liberal arts school. At Waterloo, a cooperative education format had been introduced decades back and had been refined as perhaps the most advanced mathematical and engineering school for practical and academic learning on the continent. Steve majored in mathematics, with a minor in computer science, while Peter and Mike majored in engineering – Pete as a mechanical engineer and Mike as a computer engineer.

The program had each student attend classes for eight straight month. Then the student commenced a first work term at some business. Work terms covered Canada, the United States, Asia and Europe. Very recently Steve made a trip up from Texas with some colleagues, to do recruiting on campus at the University of Waterloo, looking for new graduates who might be lured to their company in Texas. Steve's Texas compadres were astounded to find that the University has a whole building devoted to just conducting interviews. The program after the first work term became cyclical. Four month of school, followed by four months of work, followed by four months of school and so on. The program requires five years to complete a degree, but in that time each student has had two full years of work experience. Unlike some schools who schedule an internship for the last few months of a senior year, these students learn from their work, carry that learning back to their classes, which helps to focus them on their learning experience.

The co-op program also helps to fund their education. Helen and I paid for each son to finish their first eight-month term. Then the University through its extensive partnerships with corporations placed them in a work term suited to the studies being pursued. With each work term, each son earned approximately $10,000 to $12,000. This money had to support them with housing and living costs during the work term, and also had to be set aside to pay for tuition and living expenses during the next school term. Helen and I often had to "top up" a son nearing the end of a school term that was running out of money and needed funds for food and rent, but rarely more than $1000 or $1500 at a time. Helen and I had a goal for our children, that each child either graduate from university debt free, or whatever student loans they may have incurred, I would able to pay for them upon graduation. This was a unique challenge for me, because when Helen and I were having fun making babies, we never stepped back to realize that one summer were going to have four teenagers. Nor did we consider the fact that one year we would have three children in university simultaneously, and four years with at least two children in school. God provided for us well, and we were able to realize our goal. What we did not learn until I believe only Mike was left in school, was that the children were also taking care of each other. When one child was in a work term, and one in a school term, the working brother was giving money to the brother in classes to help them over financial humps.

This care for each other extended beyond school. Several years later, Amy was working for a major corporation in downtown Toronto. She lived not far from the city centre, and used bus and subway for her daily commute. Looking for a more challenging environment she sought and won a job working for a company located in west Toronto near the airport. Toronto is perhaps the only major city in the world that does not have adequate public transportation from its city centre to its international airport, but such is the case. I was living and working in Ohio, and Steve called me one evening to talk about Amy's new job. "She is going to need a car," Steve said. "I know," I replied "and I am worried about her buying someone else's castoff and inheriting problems. I wish she could afford a new car." "Have you got anything in mind?" Steve asked. "I have been looking at these new Dodge Neons, and have read good things about them." I should make full disclosure here, and state that my father worked for Chrysler Corporation for 38 years. Hence my attention to a Chrysler product for Amy. "How much would one cost," asked Steve. "I think somewhere in the neighbourhood of $20,000 to $21,000" I replied. "I'll split it with you" Steve said. I sat momentarily stunned. Steve was well situated in Texas with a company that paid him a handsome salary, but the fact that he was willing to contribute in excess of $10,000 dollars to his sister simply because she needed a car was hard to grasp. I breathed a silent prayer "Thank you Helen…" and then suggested to Steve that since it was Amy's life and her car, that we include her in the conversation. In the end we split the cost of the car three ways, between Amy, Steve and I, to allow Amy to begin building up financial credit history.

This same loving, caring and willingness to help attitude was shared by all of our kids and when a Texas clinical trial surfaced on the horizon our kids were ready. All of our children are goal oriented people, and not surprisingly all four have wound up in positions of responsibility within their companies, carrying either a manager or director title. With respect to Helen and I they are also very goal oriented and encouraged us in a multitude of ways. With Helen's illness came considerable frustration for them. In their work roles, they were accustomed to making things happen. They were very angry at this disease, and they wanted to attack it in any way possible. Getting angry at something intangible like a disease does not yield the same satisfaction as getting angry at a person or an object. But, they were prepared to fight. Amy, Mike and Lian began to spend as many weekends with us in Chatham as possible. They began to take on responsibilities around the house, doing physical tasks like yard work, house cleaning, grocery shopping and so on. Helen had begun to lose weight with her illness and the girls took her shopping for new clothes, always picking up the tab. It almost seemed to me like Helen was a big doll and the girls were having fun dressing her up. In the almost 10 years with his first company, Steve had done an inordinate amount of travel, and had "points" accumulated with virtually every hotel chain, had over a million miles with one airline and significant mileage points with others.

Steve became the guy on the ground for the Dallas trips. He booked airplane flights. He booked hotels. He booked restaurants. What he negotiated with his accumulated points and what he paid for out of his own pocket we were never allowed to know, and I still do not know to this day. All I know is that when Helen arrived at the Dallas airport with some family member in tow, Steve was there to meet us/them, ready to chauffer us to the hotel, and ready to take us out to dinner. When I would offer to pay for something, Steve would say "I cannot do anything that will make Mom better, but I can organize trips and be responsible for logistics. It's taken care of." By this time I was beginning to experience a dizziness and vertigo problem which has been ascribed to both inner ear problems and severe anemia, and which is still under investigation by an internist. As a result, I did not accompany Helen on all trips. Amy accompanied her on one trip, Mike accompanied Helen and I on a second trip, and her sister Carol accompanied Helen and Amy on yet another trip. The first trip was primarily assessment, lab work, reviewing scan information provided by Dr. Hamm in Canada, and much, much discussion about the process and what Helen could anticipate experiencing.

Helen went to these visits with her head held high ready to endure any treatment.

In her treatments back in Canada, Dr. Hamm had promised Helen that she would never be sick. Dr. Hamm administered anti-nausea drugs before, during and after treatments, and true to her word, Helen was not once sick. I was with Helen on her second trip to Dallas, when she received her first treatment. Because of the strength and amount of the actual chemo she was to receive, the doctors feared that her liver could not process that chemical shock plus the potent anti-nausea meds, so Helen agreed to proceed with significantly reduced anti-nausea medication. The chemo treatment was made early in the morning. It seemed to go well, but shortly after 2:00 PM as Steve and Mike were having lunch in the building cafeteria, and as Helen was resting in a recovery room, she was suddenly violently ill. She fled to a washroom and for the next three hours experienced constant vomiting and diarrhea. I felt so helpless as I mopped her sweaty brow with a cold washcloth, watched the contortions of her body, and ran interference for her as she rushed time and time again to the washroom. In all of our married life together I had never seen anything like this. In her worst moments of morning sickness with pregnancies or with bouts of the flu, I had never seen her body convulsed in this way. It was as if a demon of some kind had taken over control of her body. Around 5:00 PM Helen was given what looked like a small dishpan, in case of further vomiting, and brought down to the entry door in a wheelchair. Steve had pulled his car right up to the entrance and helped Helen into the car. Just as we were leaving the nurse gave Helen an anti-nausea medication. After each chemo treatment, Helen was given a secondary injection within 24 hours of treatment to help maintain her white blood count. Helen's treatment was on Wednesday, and we had planned to fly back to Detroit on Thursday, so that the medication could be administered on Friday. When we reached the hotel room, the anti-nausea medication had kicked in, and Helen fell into a fitful sleep for five hours. It was obvious we were not travelling to Detroit the next day, and our logistics expert Steve simply made it so. Hotel rooms were extended, flights were rescheduled and Helen was able to have a restful day Thursday, most of it spent in sleep. When she, Mike and I returned to Chatham on the Friday, she simply missed the WBC medication.

It was agreed by all medical people concerned, that Helen would have two treatments in Dallas, and then a CT scan to see if the medication was working. If it was not doing its job, Helen would be dropped from the trial and would come back under Dr. Hamm's treatment arsenal in Windsor. After what Helen experienced with her first treatment, I have no idea from where she mustered the courage to get back on a plane three weeks later to go have her body abused again. Amy and Carol accompanied her; the return trip was planned for the Friday. After a telephone consultation with Dr. Hamm, it was decided that Helen must have the white blood count medication which must be received within the 24 hour window. On Friday while Helen, Carol and Amy were flying north, I went to the Windsor hospital pharmacy and picked up the syringe. My cousin Judy, a retired nurse met us at the house within minutes of the girls completing the drive from Detroit to Chatham on Friday evening, and administered the injection, well within the time limit.

I should add here, that Helen was being cared for not only by the medical community. With each visit to Dallas, Kristen and Steve brought "Team Texas" to Dallas with them from Austin. Travelling with three pre-schoolers, one of which was an infant and one only one year old is not a simple task. Three child seats required in the back of the car; all of the clothes, diapers, bottles, baby food and essentials for any unforeseen event must be transported. Kristen did her best to keep the children on schedule and entertained in hotel rooms, but she knew that Helen needed the warmth of the love of her "chosen daughter" and grandchildren in addition to the medical treatments.

Tuesday, February 2, 2010

Update February 2, 2010

I can report for both of us that things are continuing to go well. David had a check-up visit yesterday in London for his eye surgery and the doctor was pleased - as is David - with the continuing healing and improvement in his vision. Next visit is in 3 months, so all is going well. He is even starting to be able to read again with his right eye - large letters, but he can now see them and is quite encouraged. You value your eyesight but when it is threatened, you learn to value it even more.

I had my second chemo dose a week ago (Monday, Jan. 25) and, once again, it was a non-event. This is a different type of chemical than the first round a year ago and my body seems to tolerate it very well...it's like nothing has actually happened, believe it or not. I have really good anti-nausea meds, including a steroid that I am to take for the first 3 days after I have my 'dose', morning and evening. This time around, I didn't need to take the evening ones and I felt fine. I was out for lunch, dinner and breakfast during the week, did all my usual jobs around the house and so on. I continue, thankfully, to be able to lead a normal life and wake up in the morning feeling good. I am waiting to see if/when I will lose my lovely new gray hair - not my favourite part of all of this. I have been able to purchase a gray wig (not too many of those around!) and will take it to my excellent hairdresser for her magic touch. There are two family weddings this year, August and October, and I am already calculating whether or not I will have my own hair for them !

This treatment is the one that will decide the future course of action. I will have a CT scan Feb. 12 and, on the basis of those results, we will decide whether or not to continue treatment in Windsor or contact Dallas for screening to be admitted to the clinical trial there. Treatment in Windsor would finish in mid-April; treatment in Dallas would mean going every 3 weeks for a period of time I do not know at this point. Nice to have the options; hard to know what would be the right thing to do. Fortunately, I have confidence that God will make my way plain to me and others. Sometimes it's hard to say things like that - I want to know the whole story, including the ending, right now !! (Those of you who know me well know that I often read the end of a novel to see if I like it before I read the whole thing...

it's also a way for me to be able to put the book down and not read the whole thing at once!) But it gives me practice in trusting God and praying the prayer that never fails - "Thy will be done". This is an ongoing lesson for me.

I meet so many friends, neighbours and acquaintances who tell me "I pray for you every day". I thank you for that so much; it's what gives me strength to get up in the morning and live my day and not waste time agonizing over this illness. I have today, like everyone else, and I live it and enjoy it. I like to think that the people who are praying for me are one of the positive results of this disease - some are praying who haven't for a while and it's good for them to get back in the habit !! God does really work in mysterious ways.

Well, that's about all the news from here. I hope that your day goes well and that God will give you His peace and strength to deal with whatever comes your way today.

Tuesday, February 9, 2010

Update - February 9, 2010

I'm happy to report that things are continuing to go well for both of us. David's eyesight continues to improve on a daily basis. I have returned to my line dancing class (beginner!) and have made it through both of the classes so far without having to sit and rest hardly at all - much better than I was before Christmas. I have also joined the YMCA and got through my introductory hour of practice exercises, treadmill and bike with no problem. Both of these experiences make me feel quite hopeful that the chemo is doing its job. However...you know the rest - also trying not to get too hopeful. Also doing all the normal life things - making it to church, going out for lunches and so on, knitting a blanket for my newest granddaughter, reading, cooking, grocery shopping, etc. So, as I said, things are going well.

Next event is the CT scan this Friday (Feb. 12) and then the visit with my oncologist on Tuesday, Feb. 16. After that, the path will be clearer.

Thank you all again for your ongoing prayers, support, cards and encouragement. They mean more than I can express.

Thursday, February 18, 2010

Update - February 18, 2010

Well, Tuesday brought no answers, in spite of expectations. The CT scan results were not available and although my oncologist had the images on her laptop, she didn't feel that she could interpret them accurately. So - I went ahead with the chemo treatment (#3) scheduled that day. We waited in her office for an hour while she waited for radiology to send the images but there was no 'reading' to go with them. Next scheduled visit is March 8, with chemo on

March 9. If information on the CT scan comes through, she will send it to me but it looks like any decision will be made now March 8 about whether or not to continue this treatment, based on its effectiveness. This was especially disappointing, as my daughter had taken a day off work to accompany us. However, we were glad of her company, regardless.

Please pray for me that I will have courage to deal with the information that comes from the CT scan and the wisdom to make good decisions about future treatment that will be based on that. I met a charming and stylish lady in the chemo department while I was being 'dosed' who told me she had been on chemo more or less for 3 years and had not had any hair for all of that time...gives one perspective but also a vision of other possibilities, which can be unnerving.

I have to keep remembering that we are given the gift of today and that it is ours to use and enjoy. Tomorrow is not guaranteed to anyone. Today it is sunny, my head cold seems to be letting up, my children are all hanging in there with their various challenges and still have time to check up on me, my husband's eyesight is improving all the while, my sister has passed the first anniversary of her terrible fall and is renovating her kitchen - lots of things to be thankful for! It's a choice, so often and I am following a friend's advice to "Choose joy!" It's much easier to live with.

Hope your day goes well and that you find your own joy in it.

Wednesday, February 24, 2010

Update February 24, 2010

Well, I got the results yesterday from the CT scan Feb. 12 and it wasn't good news - it shows 'a progression of the disease' . My oncologist intends to change me over to a different type of chemo when I see her again March 8 or 9. It was a shock to hear that, since I have felt so well - apart from the terrible chest cold that David and I have both been fighting since Valentine's. (I am on an antibiotic, too, because I also had chemo Feb. 16).

David and I have decided that I will try to get a screening appointment in Dallas to see if I can be admitted to the Phase 2 trial there that we were able to investigate in December. I don't know what will come of it but I think it is an opportunity that came to me, unlooked for, and that I should follow up on.

Hard to know what to do...pretty scary as well. It just does not seem possible that I could be dealing with this when my life seems so normal. You would never know to see me that I have anything like this going on inside of me. No symptoms, no pain, no shortness of breath, etc. I can do pretty well anything that I want to do - drive, get groceries, cook meals, read, knit, etc. If it wasn't for this cold, I would be 'in good health', to all appearances.

Harder today to say "Thy will be done", "It's in God's hands", "God will care for me" but these are all still true.

Thank you again for your prayers and support.

Friday, March 5, 2010

Update - March 5, 2010

There has been a lot happen since the last post ! I began the process of going to Dallas right after I received the news about the CT scan and a week ago today, Feb. 26, the pieces fell into place for me to go. I flew to Dallas Monday, March 1, had my screening appointment Tuesday, March 2 and flew back home Wednesday, March 3. I have also had a chance to discuss my CT scan with my family doctor on Thursday, March 4. A huge bonus to all of this was that my son who lives in Texas and his family all came to meet me in Dallas and I had time with him, my dear daughter-in-law and my three 'grands'. So, as you can see, it's been quite a week.

The experience in Dallas was very informative. We had over 2 hours in the Research Center and received a lot of information. I can be admitted to that trial if I so choose. If I do, I need to return there March 16 to start, and will continue to go there every three weeks as long as the treatment is working. Since it is a private research center, most of the financial costs would be covered by the foundation or the sponsoring drug company. I would be responsible for my own travel and accommodation costs. They were very OK with getting anything medical done in Ontario that I could and just having the information sent to them - blood work, CT scans, etc. So - it all looks good. It would be a big expense in physical effort though for me

- I found the week tiring and I didn't have any stray chemicals floating around to deal with. The nurse-practitioner who was speaking with us said that a clinical trial with a drug called a PARP-1 Inhibitor would be the best type of trial for my kind of breast cancer but that they weren't doing anything with them. (My oncologist had already told me this too.) She also advised trying experimental drugs first, because they have very specific criteria as to who can be admitted to the trials; I am already excluded from a trial for a PARP-1 drug that my oncologist knew about because I had started on the carboplatin. The 'standard of care' drugs can be held in reserve for later in the process because they are known quantities - it's known what they will do. So - lots of information, no clear path to a decision as yet.

My family doctor more or less seconded this advice yesterday, regarding the clinical trials and advised me to keep as many options open as possible for a long as possible. The progression shown in the CT scan is not measurable apparently - just identifiable. I still feel that this is the most bizarre experience of my life. I look perfectly normal and healthy - good colour, can do normal things, etc. and yet there is apparently this disease growing inside me. It's extremely difficult to reconcile the two and make the plans that are necessary for the future. When I retired, one of my goals at the top of my 'To Do' list was to clean out this house - 35 years' worth of 'stuff' accumulated from children now gone, parents' homes after they left us, school papers, etc. - and I still want to do that. It seems even more urgent now and involves so many decisions that will be hard to make.

On a brighter note, the time I had with my Texans was very enjoyable. Baby Emmy is filled out, bright-eyed and energetic and gives those wonderful baby grins. It was so good to see this 'preemie' doing so well. Lily and Clay were happy to see me although Lily still isn't really sure who I am and they were not sure why they found me in a hotel in Dallas, but apart from that, we had a good visit. Steve and Kristen continue to be the amazing, loving support that they have always been - I am very blessed.

This weekend is a big birthday bash - we had to postpone the celebration for David's 65th birthday on Feb. 26 since he and I both had terrible chest colds. It turned out to be a good decision because the weather was also terrible. Plans are to celebrate this Saturday, which is also our youngest son's birthday, so we can do 2 for 1. Three out of our four kids will be here and at least two of them will come to Windsor to my appointment with my oncologist on Monday morning.

That will be another big decision day - we have our input from Dallas and my doctor will have her options to discuss with us. I will have to decide whether or not to proceed with the option in Dallas or one of the other options that will come up. As I said earlier, the best thing (I think - but I'm not the expert here) would be to get into a clinical trial for a PARP-1 Inhibitor drug, since it seems to be having a lot of success with triple-negative breast cancer, but I don't have information on one that I could qualify for. I am booked for chemo on Tuesday, March 9 but if I choose to take the option in Dallas, I might not be able to do that. So - We would appreciate prayer that the decision will be clear to make. There is no 'right' or 'wrong' choice - nobody knows what will work and what won't - it's all trial and error, since each person and each cancer responds in its own way.

It's getting harder to be positive and calm in the face of all this - I have had some really bad days in the last two weeks and have been very frightened of what the future might hold. However, I have fought my way back to my conviction that God is in this with me and is preparing the way for me in all things. There are just so many little confirmations - the man I met on the plane on the way back from Dallas, who told me about his brother-in-law's cancer and how positive he was about it, and who urged me to 'pray for guidance and keep on fighting'...the friend who called as I was just going out the door to the airport Monday that I hadn't talked to for months who 'just felt she had to call' and who encouraged me as I was starting out on the trip...my son who took days off work to be with me in Dallas...I am sent lots of help, often from people I do not know.

My sister advised me to read the Psalms and I found this in Psalm 116:" Death stared me in the face - I was frightened and sad. (I thought - Yeah ! That's me, alright!) Then I cried, 'Lord, save me!' How kind He is! How good He is! So merciful, this God of ours. The Lord protects the simple and childlike; I was facing death and He saved me. Now I can relax. (Still working on that!) For the Lord had done this wonderful miracle for me. He saved me from death, my eyes from tears and my feet from stumbling. I shall live ! Yes, in His presence - here on earth."

I do not know how it will all turn out but I know who will be with me and going ahead of me to prepare the way and I just have to not forget that.

May your day be a good one ! Thank you again for your interest, support and prayers. They are always appreciated.

Wednesday, March 10, 2010

Update - March 10, 2010

Once again, a lot has happened since the last time I wrote.

First of all, we had a wonderful weekend celebrating birthdays and just being together as a family. We were expecting three out of the four kids but were VERY pleasantly surprised when

#4, "the Big Guy", stepped out of the car Saturday afternoon as well. So, we were able to celebrate 3 out of the 6 family birthdays and just really enjoyed our time together. It was a real gift to be all together again so soon after Christmas and probably won't happen again until Pete and Jocelyn's wedding in Seattle in August.

On Monday, five of us set out for my oncologist appointment in Windsor. As you know, I was praying so much for a clear direction as a result of that meeting and many of you were praying that for us as well - thank you again. That is what we got. My oncologist strongly recommended that I take the option open to me in Dallas and we could all see that it was the best choice for me at this point. We also received the radiologist report on my CT scan of Feb. 12 which shows that the cancer is progressing in spite of the carboplatinum treatments - not good news. Some of the nodules are stable, but some are growing - in millimetres, but growing. What I am looking for now and praying for is a drug that will stop the growth and possibly even shrink these nodules and tumours that are there. Hopefully, that is what I will find in Dallas. I keep reminding myself that this was an option that came to me unlooked for and I am trusting that it is God's plan for me.

David and I and our youngest son will leave for Dallas Monday, March 15. I should have the first treatment of either the experimental drug or the control drug on Tuesday, a second check-up on Wednesday and then fly back home Thursday. Once I start, I will be going there every three weeks. I still have to have this confirmed, so it is possible that there will be some changes to this schedule.

David also has some medical issues happening - he has been troubled by dizziness when he stands and begins to walk to the point where he has fallen several times. He will be having some tests done for this as well - we are both falling apart !!!

That is about all for now - will keep you updated as things develop. I am looking forward to the opportunities in Dallas and praying that there will be good results from whatever I am treated with there. Please pray that I - and the rest of the family - will be able to trust God in this and stay in the peace of that confidence instead of distressing ourselves with the 'what ifs' and bad possibilities.

Post a Comment On: <u>Helen's Journal</u>
Martha said...

Dear Helen,

So happy to hear that you had a great weekend with your children. We continue to think positive and keep you and your family in our thoughts and prayers. Safe journey to Texas.

Love & Prayers
Martha and Jack

Monday, March 22, 2010

Update - March 22, 2010

Well, at the risk of being repetitious - there's still a lot going on ! March is passing in a blur.

First of all, David found out on March 12, that there's nothing wrong with his heart or blood pressure - the dizziness and falling are the result of problems with his inner ear. It's a type of vertigo and he returned from his doctor's appointment with a simple head-over-the-end-of-the-bed exercise that he can repeat several times a week to 're-set' his balance mechanism. He has seen a remarkable improvement even in a few days and feels much more confident and sure of his mobility. We were very relieved to discover the cause and to have a simple solution for the problem ! He has more tests scheduled but this was a big result. While all this was happening, I was cooling my heels in Windsor, going through the process of another CT scan.

On Monday, March 15, our youngest son arrived from Kitchener to accompany us and be our assist with luggage, etc. and we all flew to Dallas that evening. Tuesday was not Day 1 of treatment, as originally planned; instead, I had some of the screening blood work repeated and a couple of conversations with various people who are running the cancer centre. Mike was able to record these so that other family members could hear the discussions. I did find out that day that I was randomized into the experimental drug group - another answer to prayer !! In a way, I was not surprised - just felt that things were continuing to work out 'as planned'.

Wednesday was 'Day 1' and what a day it turned out to be. We were at the hospital for 9:00 - started getting anti-nausea meds by 9:27 and the IV treatment of the drug started about 10:27 for 2 hours. No problem there - just sit in a nice recliner and read a magazine or something while it drips into you. First blood samples were taken about 1:15 or so and I was told that I had about 2 hrs. to wait until the next one. I could go down to the atrium and get something to eat or whatever as long as I didn't leave the building. Well, I made it to the waiting room and realized that I wasn't leaving the office! I returned to a treatment room with a bed and checked out until about 2:15, when the reactions started, as I had been warned...diarrhea for half an hour or so took care of half my digestive system. I rested until it was time for the next blood draw and returned to the chemo room - was part way through the blood draw when the nausea arrived - took care of the other part of my digestive system! I had been given anti-nausea meds at 9:27; thinking that these had worn off, they gave me more and of a different kind. This stuff just T-boned me - couldn't talk right, couldn't walk without help - doped to the gills! But I didn't throw up much afterwards! Anyhow - left the hospital about 5:30 in a wheelchair with a bucket in my lap...

returned to the hotel and slept it off until about 10:00, when I awoke starving and managed some toast. Steve was there too and brought me back to the hotel in his car, which was a lot better than a cab. We realized late that evening that I wasn't in any shape to be flying the next day, so David, Steve and Mike re-arranged things to leave Friday instead. That will have to be the plan from now on, I think.

Thursday was better; we were back to the hospital for another blood draw by 7:30 and then had time for a family breakfast at the hotel after we got back. Kristen and the grandkids had made the trip to Dallas too, so we had a nice time together. I found that my taste was off again - one of the side effects of chemo - but I could eat OK. The highlight of the day was dinner that night at a Beni Hanna restaurant (Japanese teppanyaki, where they cook at the table). We all enjoyed it, and Clay found it especially entertaining. I had a pretty good day - just had to rest in the afternoon - but no other side effects...just recovering.

Friday we were able to have one last family breakfast together before we all split up - the Austin tribe to make the return trip and the Ontario tribe to the airport. We had a later flight - left Dallas at 4:00 CT and arrived back in Detroit just after 10:00 p.m. We were in Chatham by 12:15 and Mike left to drive back to KW by 12:30 ! The night was clear and the road was almost empty, so it was a good time for him to go.

Overall, it was a good experience. I have been quite tired since returning but then I haven't had the usual 3 days post-treatment of 'happy pills' - steroids and my big anti-nausea med. So - a little more realistic, perhaps, and I have had to listen to my body more and not push it, which is probably good. However, I do feel a bit more 'settled' today and am hoping that I am over the worst of it. Time will tell ! The staff in Dallas were already talking about trying different anti-nausea meds for me next time, so we'll see what difference that might make. They are great people, very kind and sympathetic, as most people seem to be who have chosen this line of work.

I return to Dallas the week after Easter for a second treatment and then will have another CT scan April 21 to see if the drug is having any effect. If it is, then I return to Dallas for Cycle 3 the last week of April. That will be the pattern - two treatments and then a CT scan. If the results are good, then we continue. If the cancer shows growth of 20% or more, the treatments are discontinued and another plan will be drawn up. So please pray that there will be reason to continue !

I do feel that this is God's plan for me - even though I wasn't too sure there for a while about all the traveling - but it just seems so unusual that I would even have this opportunity that I don't know how else it would come about. I am so thankful that I can try this, thankful for the time to see the Austin tribe, thankful for the time with other family members - there's a lot of good coming out of this, even though it is scary. Friends feel that they would like to pray for me and they do - in coffee shops, in halls in the church, in wherever we happen to be - I am in awe of their caring and support. When I get rattled, I think back to some of these experiences and am comforted and calmed. So many of you are praying for me and for our family and I thank you so much. I have a little 'mental collection' of faces, comments, etc. that I draw on when the black thoughts swirl around in my head and they help me turn away from all of that and choose to trust, choose not to panic, choose to 'rest in the Lord'. Thank you again.

Isn't it great to see the robins back and wake up to birdsong in the mornings ? Spring is going to make it ! Choose joy !

Tuesday, March 30, 2010

Update - March 30, 2010

Welcome to my life on the couch !

It's been 2 weeks now since I had my first chemo treatment with the experimental drug in Dallas and it has affected me more than any other chemo that I have had. I think I must have been getting off easy before.

It's all there in the list of possible side effects that I was given - fatigue, reduced white and red blood cell counts, loss of appetite - but I just haven't had such a long reaction before. It's usually been a week and then I was more or less back to normal. I'm still up and dressed, etc. and doing normal household activities - laundry, cooking, groceries - but I just have to rest for 30 - 45 min. between jobs and that's frustrating... leaves me with a lot of 'bedhead' ! However, it could be worse, a lot worse, and I am trying to keep perspective. I was also quite weepy there for a while but that seems to be passing, too.

David continues to be better as the result of that exercise for his inner ear balance but he does have to keep doing it on a regular basis to keep 'level-headed'!! (Couldn't resist.)

We are looking forward to family visits this Easter weekend, including my sister from Ottawa who will accompany me to Dallas the following week for Cycle 2. Amy has to go to Dallas also for a working trip, so I will have lots of company.

I am also looking forward to Easter as a reminder again of God's amazing, incomprehensible love for mankind and of His desire to bring this love to the lives of ordinary people like you and me. It is the story of Easter that gives me hope in this battle and confidence that however it turns out, it will be God's plan and that I will be OK. Like all gifts, God's love must be received and accepted to be part of your life or it just sits there on the shelf in its wrapping paper.

Thank you again for your prayers. Choose joy!!

Post a Comment On: <u>Helen's Journal</u>
Daniel said...

Aunt Helen, I continue to uphold you in my prayers. I trust that things go well for you in your treatment down in Dallas this week. Love you lots.
Dan Jr.

Dan & Leona said...

Dear David Helen:

Don't forget, you are in our daily thoughts and prayers. Trust you have some good "grandma time" in Dallas.

Love, Dan Leona

Gail said...

Helen:

Our thoughts and prayers are with you. Hope this trip to Dallas is better than the first one. Enjoy those grandchildren. Gail

Jane & Steve said...

I have had the song "God will make a way" in my heart and head for some time over the past week. It's a promise I've been claiming, that no matter what the circumstance, what the need, God WILL make a way. I trust him in that for you and Dave.

You are never far from my thoughts and prayers,

Jane

Monday, April 5, 2010

Update - April 5, 2010

Not too much to tell but I thought I'd just bring everyone up to the present. This week is scheduled to be my second treatment in Dallas and my sister and I fly down there tomorrow. I should have the treatment on Wednesday if my blood work report is good. I'm a little anxious about it this time because I had such a strong reaction the last time...but they were going to try some other nausea meds, so we'll see how it goes. At least I know to give myself a recovery day before the return flight! Steve and Kristen are bringing the kids up again, so there is more 'grandma time' and Amy is already there on business, so we should all have supper Tuesday night, before the fun starts.

We had a lovely Easter weekend with my sister and two of our four, plus fiancée. I was able to go to the Good Friday service at church, *which was very moving. We had Easter dinner on Saturday night and the amount of effort I put into getting that ready apparently ran my system right down because I then had to spend most of Easter Sunday in bed. That is more an indication of how little energy I have these days than how much I did, because I had lots of help. I was really disappointed but I just couldn't pull it off.*

I have found this chemo to be more debilitating than any of the other kinds that I have had. I go to Dallas not feeling really recovered from the first round - another reason for my anxiety. When I read the list of 'possible side effects', I see 'tiredness', 'muscle weakness', 'decreased appetite', 'low red blood cell count' - all things that could account for this. I'll be asking about it when there. I'm also hoping that if this medicine is having this much effect on my body, then it must also be having an effect on the cancer. God continues to reassure me, through various people's comments and other ways, that He has a plan and has things under control and that I am not to worry. Some days take more practice at that than others !

That's about all there is to say, except to thank you all once again for your prayers, cards, and concern. Your kindness is so much appreciated.

Wednesday, April 14, 2010

Update - April 14, 2010

Well, things didn't quite work out as expected in Dallas.

We did go out for supper together Tuesday evening, but I have been finding that my appetite really drops off in the evening and I wasn't able to eat much of my supper. (I have lost approximately 30 pounds since Feb. 2009.) Apart from that, we had a good time. There's also the issue of what to order, because in Texas things are spiced up more than they are here and a lot of it is too spicy for me now.

I got the second treatment of the drug on Wednesday and they tried some different anti-nausea meds, so there was a bit of a change. I was sick more and had more diarrhea but it wasn't as violent as the first round. Back to the hotel and a quiet night ! It was also decided that I needed the shot I was getting the first time I had chemo, to bring my white blood cell count back up. Tests had shown that it had dropped to 500 instead of a normal 1500 with the first treatment of the Dallas medicine. That meant I had to get back to Chatham Friday - and that I also needed a chest x-ray - so plans were made Wed. evening to fly back Thursday instead of Friday. However, it became clear on Thursday that I wasn't going anywhere except back to bed, so we returned to the original Friday schedule. Back in Chatham, David was making arrangements to drive to Windsor on Friday, pick up the

Neulasta and have it here at the house when I did get home Friday evening. An RN in the family was kind enough to come over Friday night and 'shoot' me, so I did get the med. Friday after all. (Chest x-ray had to wait until today, when I also had to get blood work done in Windsor,)

I was hoping that the Neulasta would work its magic pretty quickly but I have been down again all of this week I just have very little energy, (the reason I have not done this blog until now) have trouble breathing and can only sleep on one side - although I seem to manage OK most nights. There's a reduction in the usual household chores that I can do, too - we are all seeing quite an effect from this chemo - more than we have seen with any other. I can only hope that it means that it is also having a similar effect on the cancer and wiping it out, too.

So that's where I am now - thank you so much for your prayers. Almost every day I met someone who says, "I pray for you every day"

It's both humbling and encouraging - when I get down, it's a comforting thing to remember. A friend at church gave me a little devotional book written by a minister who contracted ALS, or Lou Gehrig's disease. I have been finding it very helpful, as it addresses issues that I also deal with. The thought this morning was "You have to surrender yourself and your future to God." The idea is that you can't influence much of what is or is not going to happen to you and to spend time worrying about it and fearing it is a waste. He will provide as necessary - but often at the last minute ! Anyhow - I'm working on that - has to happen several times a day, sometimes, but it does bring a certain peace.

I hope you are enjoying this beautiful spring, as it unfolds so wonderfully around us. It speaks to me of God's reliability and His love of beautiful things - and of extravagance !

Helen's Journey

Helen mentions her shortness of breath and having to sleep on one side. She lay on one side because that was the only way she could breathe. The stairs in our home leading from the main floor to the second have thirteen steps. Helen became unable to make that accent in one pass. She could go four steps, and then had to pause, often to sit down on a step, to catch her breath. After a few minutes she could go four more steps, then another pause for breath, and then finally complete the trip. We reached the point that she would attempt to make one trip down in the morning, and one trip up in the evening, spending the bulk of her time downstairs, mostly on the couch. I became extremely concerned for her well being and finally called our family doctor to talk to his nurse about Helen's breathing problems. She in turn referred me to a local medical oxygen supply company, who immediately sent someone over for an assessment. The assessment demonstrated that Helen had a critical need for oxygen to supplement her breathing and our living room soon took on the look of a welding shop with upwards of 6-10 cylinders side by side, each good for three hours of breathing. I began to keep track of time constantly when we were out. Sitting in Sunday School Class, for example, I watched the time run down on the current cylinder from which Helen was breathing, and then when needed, would disconnect that cylinder, and quickly connect another, all the while trying not to disrupt the class. This also meant one other very significant thing: we could no longer fly as we could not take the pressurized cylinders on an airplane. We had an oxygen concentrator which sat in our living room, to which was connected a 50 hose which could reach virtually every place on the main floor and could reach upstairs to Helen's bedroom and her bathroom. That 50 foot hose and the 10 foot hose connected to the portable oxygen cylinders, became her "leash."

Monday, April 19, 2010

Update - April 19, 2010

Some interesting developments since I last wrote !

David thought that I might benefit from oxygen assistance and made arrangements for a respiratory company to come and give me an assessment last Thursday, with the result that I am now attached by a 50' hose to something called a 'oxygen concentrator'. It was making a tremendous improvement within 24 hours - I could eat more, breathe better, had better colour, and felt more 'normal'. This is not compressed oxygen, although I have a tank for that, too - only lasts 3 hours - but a compressor which condenses the oxygen in the house air and adds it to what I am already breathing at the rate of 2L per minute. Amazing again how much difference it has made! I am very appreciative and thankful that David not only thought of it but went ahead and did it. I was kind of getting to where I thought it might be a good idea but would have had a hard time making the phone call - more 'invalid' stuff. So you can picture me now with one of those little clear hose things hooked over my ears and two little prongs in my nose - and a big smile, because I feel so much better with it!

Double-edged, though - can't take this equipment through an airport or on a plane, so will now have to find some source in Dallas to rent it, because I can't manage a week without it. We'll be on the way there again a week from today and I'm wondering how I'll make it through the plane trip...just not talk for 5 hours, I guess...I didn't realize how gaspy I had gotten until I got on the O2. It's very obvious when I have to be off it. So - something good to report !

I was able, with the help of Mike and Lian (youngest son and fiancée), to attend a memorial service in London on Saturday for a dear professor of many years ago. There were many friends there that I hadn't seen for some time and they were a real blessing to me and an encouragement, even though I couldn't stay to visit for long afterwards - had to get to the car for my O2.

I am encouraged daily. We went for supper last Thursday to Swiss Chalet and ran into friends who used to live here but who moved away years ago. They were in town just for the day to visit some other people that they knew. The wife of the couple has been a spiritual mentor to me for about 40 years, so it was a very special 'accident'. We had a great time but the best part was that she asked if she could anoint me with oil before we separated, as a sign that we were mutually turning this health issue over to God. I was happy to agree - and even more so when I found that her oil was actually spikenard from Israel. God continues to bring experiences and people to me that remind me that He is involved in this and not to be afraid.

Thank you again for your prayers - there are so many of you who are so kind to remember me and I appreciate it so much.

Sunday, April 25, 2010

Update - April 25, 2010

Good morning

We received word yesterday afternoon, based on the CT scan I had last Wed., that the Texas trial drug is having no appreciable effect on my cancer and the recommendation was that I not come to Dallas this coming week or proceed with that treatment path. Instead, I will be seeing my oncologist in Windsor for the next steps. I was more relieved than anything else because I was very concerned about this upcoming trip and how I was going to be able to get through it. I have lain awake at night trying to figure out how many of these treatments I could manage - 2 more? 4 more? It has been difficult and I am not really sorry that it is done. I thought it might be some miraculous controller against this thing, but apparently not. So now I will go on a 'standard of care' drug for while, I think. I am still on waiting lists in Dallas for upcoming trials but I need something else fairly quickly - it's been 5 months without anything being effective.

While it was not welcome news, I find that I am OK with it and am looking forward to talking with my oncologist on Tuesday. Amy is here and has cancelled her trip to Dallas to be with us this week. She will be with us on Tuesday and Steve may come up as well. Mike and Lian plan to be here next week and if Pete wasn't on his way home from Brazil next Tuesday, he'd probably show up too. I tell you, it makes for a full examination room when we see the doctor ! If you live in BlackBerry land, you can record conversations (with permission) on your phone and then send them to other family members who couldn't be there. I imagine that will be happening Tuesday as well.

So - I'll be here next week after all. May God be with you today.

Chapter Eight

The Bottom of the Valley

"Yeh though I walk through the valley of the shadow of death, I will fear no evil, for Thou are with me." Psalm 23. What a wonderful promise. What hope. How hard to really believe this when you are actually walking along the bottom of the valley!

Thursday, April 29, 2010

Update - April 29, 2010

Things are moving fairly quickly, so I am just going to lay it out, day by day.

Monday, we were able to have a conference call with the medical team in Dallas, to go over their decision with me. As part of that discussion, I was e-mailed my last CT scan results and the answer is plain; the main tumour on my right lung grew from 4 cm to 6 cm in the 6 weeks that I was on the experimental drug. It is now growing around my trachea, and pulmonary arteries and veins - not a good situation. The Dallas team recommended several possible chemo options and the option of radiation - within 10 days to 2 weeks and sooner if possible. We made notes to take with us to Windsor Tuesday.

Tuesday - I had an appointment with my oncologist; only David and Amy and I were going. We took a copy of our notes from Monday's conversation but it turned out that several of the drugs [the Dallas team] mentioned (Abraxane, Gemcitibine) were not covered in Ontario; the Alimta she did not feel would be effective for me. Instead, she recommended Navelbine and had made arrangements for me to have two treatments, Thursday April 29 and Thursday May 6, with a follow-up app't. and chest x-ray May 18th. I asked her for her opinion on whether or not I would be able to attend two family weddings this year - one in Seattle in August ([she replied] have a contingency plan) and one here in Ontario in October (she just put her hand on my knee and shook her head; it was clear that it wasn't just the wedding I wasn't going to make it to - pretty big shock for all concerned right there!). She feels that the cancer is becoming chemo-refractive - doesn't respond to chemo and, based on the speed with which the tumour is growing, that was a reasonable timeline. We went sadly off to do the End of Treatment things that Dallas required - blood labs, EKG and chest x-ray. When we got home, there was a phone call telling me to be in Windsor Wed. at 11:00 for my radiation consultation.

Wednesday - back to Windsor again to see a radiation oncologist. We had just started the conversation when I mentioned that I had had a chest x-ray done the day before; this was news to him and he left to look at it. When he returned, he had looked at my CT scan as well (Apr. 21). The conclusion of the discussion was that I would have 5 radiation treatments. He took my dates for my chemo in the discussion. He seemed quite positive and felt that the radiation had a good chance (50%) of stabilizing or possibly even shrinking the tumour so that I could breathe more easily. After we left him, we went up to talk to my oncologist's receptionist because I had 2 appointments booked with her - May 10 and May 18 - and wondered if I needed to keep both. In the time that it took us to go up the elevator, the radiation doctor had called her to say that he felt the radiation should take precedence over the chemo and she had agreed. So as of today, I will have 5 radiation treatments

May 3 - 7, and then see my oncologist May 10, as well as have another chest x-ray that day. The radiation doctor mentioned that the radiation could inflame my esophagus and I might have problems swallowing for a short time - not a lot of fun.

So it has been quite a week so far and there are plenty of emotions and tears swirling around the house. We had another of those family conference phone calls Tuesday night to bring everyone out of town up to date, especially about my likely not being at either wedding - more tears. So hard not to second-guess yourself - what if I had done x ? What if I hadn't done x ? Why me? Why now ? What good will come out of this ? Harder and harder to be calm and trust in the goodness of God and say "Thy will be done." Mostly, I am just saying, "NO! NO!NO!NO!"

Please pray for all of us - it's a tough week here.

Wednesday, May 5, 2010

Update - May 5, 2010

It's Cinqo de Mayo, for those of you who have Mexican connections !

(Mexican Independence Day)

I left you in a big funk last week but I am able to tell you that the clouds have cleared somewhat and I am feeling a little more positive. A few sunny days and some time thinking over all the blessings that have already come to me and I am less upset. So much of this is opinion, not fact - nobody but God knows what will happen and when. The radiologist is quite hopeful that he can have an effect on the big tumour - stabilize it or even shrink it, which would be fantastic. There are other smaller 'spots' on both lungs and that's where the next chemo will come in. My greatest prayer is that they will respond to it; the last two chemos have had no effect.

I am still on oxygen; our living room looks like a welder's supply. I can have up to 6 tanks of compressed oxygen there - using at least one every day to go to Windsor - and then there is the condenser, humming away at the foot of the stairs. I get that 50' hose tangled up a different way every day ! But it does make it easier to breathe.

I have had 3/5 radiation treatments - last two on Thursday and Friday of this week. Then I have follow-up appointments the week of June 21 (x-ray) and July 5 (to see what the effects of the radiation have been.) Monday, May 10th, I see my oncologist again for what I hope will be a discussion about the chemo. I have to have another chest x-ray that morning before that appointment - getting to be a weekly occurrence. My rib cage will be glowing in the dark before long...

Mike and Lian are here this week; Amy went home for a few days but returned last night.

Steve and my sister are arriving Friday and Pete and Jocelyn are going to be here Sat. and Sun. Everyone leaves Sunday evening or Monday morning except Amy; Mike and Lian return the next weekend for two weeks. So David and I are well looked after ! I cook my breakfast some mornings, but that's it. I haven't worried about lunch or dinner for weeks. Feels pretty good ! Some people live like that all the time !

There's a verse that struck my attention in July 2008, when I was first diagnosed. It keeps showing up - arrived in a card this week again. I'm trying so hard to keep it in mind and keep out of the 'pit of despair'. "For I the Lord thy God, will hold thy right hand, saying unto thee, Fear not; I will help thee." Isaiah 41:13. I have no idea how many times He has reached into my life and helped me in ways I don't realize in the last 22 months; I can recognize some of them and I need to remember them and be comforted, instead of childishly crying, "But what are You doing NOW?" He will work in His own time and His own way for what is best for me. Of course, some of the biggest blessings and help is the time the kids are prepared to spend with us and support us - every time I had to go to Dallas, I knew Steve and Kristen were waiting at the other end; Mike and Lian come here and cook wonderful meals, clean and keep us company, as does Amy; Pete calls regularly, as he travels on a two-week cycle between Brazil and Seattle. Medicine and supplements appear, tasty treats 'Mom likes', - David and I are just basking in all this love, and what greater blessing is there than that? Sometimes you miss what is right in front of you.

So - is that better ??? Thanks to all of you who prayed that I'd get my wheels under me again, and for the many cards of encouragement and calls that came this past week. It was a pretty black cloud but it's moved away somewhat and today was a good day.

Post a Comment On: **Helen's Journal**
Carl & Marianne said...

Helen,

It is good to know that you count your blessings and look at life with a positive attitude. I want you to know you are in our thoughts and prayers.

When I think of you and Dave, I see your gift of giving, loving, laughing, exploring,... I can't forget that grin and smile you have. Mostly I can't forget about the time we came up for your anniversary and celebrated it with your children and grand children!

We miss all of you and hope to see you sometime. We are empty nesters but we never forget our friends from Canada!!!

May God see you through these tough times and that He will give you the courage to be strong!!

God bless you all,

Carl & Marianne

Gail said...

Helen, once again you have ministered to those of us reading your blog. I am sure that you have times when you lose the feeling that God is looking after things but you always seem to overcome those feelings and find hope and peace in the situation. I hope you have a wonderful weekend with all the family and I hope they realize what a wonderful Mother/Mother-in-law/Grandmother/Sister they have.

God Bless

Gail

It's pretty dark and gloomy in the bottom of the valley. Helen and I alternated between smiles and tears, between bad days and good days. Helen at one point joked that at least we alternated. When she was having a bad day often I was having a good day and could cheer her up. And when I was wading hopelessly in the slough of despond most times she was having a good day and could throw me a rope and pull me out. The topic that often came to our lips was the upcoming weddings of our children. There was no way that Helen and I could fly to Seattle for Peter and Jocelyn's wedding in August, and Dr. Hamm had made it pretty clear that she did not expect Helen to still be alive in October for Mike and Lian's 10/10/10 wedding. Peter who works in the aerospace industry had put out proposals on behalf of his company to Embraer, an airplane manufacturing company in Brazil. Interest was high in a couple of his proposals, and he was flitting back and forth – two weeks in Brazil then two weeks in Seattle. Repeat as necessary! How were he and Jocelyn to plan a wedding?

Like everything else associated with Helen's illness, the kids faced this challenge head on. Jocelyn and Peter initially considered a wedding here in Chatham, but the restrictions of Homeland Security following 9/11 required anyone crossing the Canadian/USA border to have a passport. Many of Jocelyn's family did not have one, and the wait times to get one processed were too long in the light of the urgency of Helen's circumstances. Jocelyn's parents and sister were so accommodating and helpful. Jocelyn's Mom is very artistic, and had great plans for decorations and special effects for the wedding. Now everything would have to be redesigned, and made portable to transport somewhere. Finally, Jocelyn and Pete decided to have their wedding at the Omni Hotel in Detroit, just a few hundred yards upstream from the Renaissance Center on the banks of the Detroit River. Their new date was to be June 19th, 2010. Mike and Lian were able to obtain their originally planned locale, the same caterer, same photographer and same disk jockey in Kitchener, and moved their date up from October 10th, to June 26th. Peter and Jocelyn were able to work out their details by telephone calls and e-mail back and forth to Brazil or during their brief times together between trips.

This meant that family and friends who travelled to Detroit for the June 19th wedding had the option of remaining in the area for the June 26th wedding. This meant that Kristen and Steve had only one trip with their family instead of two. This is not as simple as it sounds, because between hotel accommodations in Detroit, in Chatham, in Kitchener and in Niagara Falls where they took the children for a mini-vacation, their rug rats slept in 10 different hotel rooms in 15 days. What troopers! What consideration by both our son and our chosen daughter Kristen to make this happen. Mike and Lian asked my brother Dan, a retired minister in British Columbia if he would perform their ceremony. Jocelyn and Peter's officiant was able to come with them from Seattle.

What a setting. A gorgeous sunny day with big white clouds on the lawn between the hotel and the Detroit River. There is a unique blue colour to the water of Lake Huron, Georgian Bay, the St. Clair River, Lake St. Clair and the Detroit River before it gets muddied into the not so blue water of Lake Erie. The green of the grass, the blue of the water, the sunshine all combined with the apple green and black colours of the ladies' dresses and the men's tuxedos melded beautifully. Jocelyn's Mom, Martha, had brought huge letters in black and sparkly silver which spelled out the word " Love" as a backdrop instead of an altar. Clay and Jackson, Jocelyn's two year old nephew, were dressed in smart black shorts complete with black suspenders, white shirts, jaunty black caps and black & white saddle shoes as Clay said to perform the role of "ring buriers." Lily was dressed in an apple green and black tutu to be the flower girl, and the dressmaker in Utah who made her dress, sent an identical one for baby Emmy. A picture perfect setting. The lakes and rivers I mentioned above are all part of the St. Lawrence seaway, funneling ships from around the world through the St. Lawrence River, through Lakes Ontario and Erie, through the Welland Canal bypassing Niagara Falls, and ultimately as far as Thunder Bay at the far end of Lake Superior or Chicago at the bottom of Lake Michigan. There are unique freighters built expressly to navigate the lakes, with their frequent and violent storms, and there are the ocean freighters recognizable by their different shape and construction. During the course of the wedding two lake freighters passed by. Seeing a wedding in progress many of the crew ran to the rail to wave while the boat whistles drowned out anything happening on land. Jocelyn and Pete and their attendants turned and waved to the ships while everyone took a brief pause until their voices could once again be heard. This was not the only nice thing that happed with the relocation. Jocelyn's 93 year old grandmother was able to be driven by one of her sons up from Kentucky to be present. She might not have been able to have made the airplane trip to Seattle. It turned into primarily a family wedding, since friends from Seattle could not make the trip. Thus it was small and intimate, and Jocelyn and Peter have subsequently had a reception in Seattle on their originally planned date, and reaffirmed their vows.

Having the wedding in Detroit meant that my brother and his wife from British Columbia, my sister and her husband from Minnesota, and Helen's sister from Ottawa were able to be present for both weddings.

Mike and Lian's wedding a week later was no less impressive. Lian is a fashion designer, and made her own wedding dress(es). She actually made three before she decided she was happy with the third one. In addition, the previous November Lian and Mike had travelled to Thailand and Laos with her father and other family members, and Lian had purchased material in Thailand to make a traditional Thai wedding dress, complete with gold accents woven through the cloth. For the wedding ceremony, she wore her "Western" dress against Mike's black tux. Then for the reception she changed into her Thai wedding dress, resplendent against Mike's white dinner jacket. Lian also make all of her attendants dresses in a lovely plum colour. Mike not being bound by tradition had asked a female friend whom he had known all through secondary school, university and in the work world to be one of his attendants. There was some consideration to having Laura wear a tuxedo, but Lian prevailed, making a dress in black to match the men, but cut to the style of the bridesmaids dresses. Mike, at the reception, nervously addressed Lian's father and her family in the Thai language, thanking the father for the gift of his daughter and for welcoming him into their family. We English speakers did not know what he said, but it seemed to be OK since the family responded with laughter and tremendous applause. Months earlier when Mike wanted to ask the father's permission to marry his daughter (I raised very traditional sons) Mike studied hard to make the request in Thai. One evening at dinner in January of 2009, just a few months before Lian's Mom succumbed to her own battle with cancer, Mike carefully asked the question he had memorized. Before Lian's father could respond, her mother from the other end of the table shouted "Yes! Yes! Yes!" So although Khem could not be with us in person she was certainly present in spirit, and we all knew how happy she had been at the prospect of Mike becoming her son through marriage to her daughter.

The radiation treatments that Dr. Hirmiz had recommended were very successful. A follow-up CT scan showed that the tumour in Helen's right lung had been reduced by almost 50%. Breathing was much easier, although Helen remained on her oxygen. As we approached the wedding dates, she felt better and better. It cost me the price of two dresses but on both wedding days, she looked radiant. She told me that she wanted her children to remember how good she looked on their wedding days, and not how sick she looked. She succeeded beyond her wildest expectation.

Wednesday, May 12, 2010

Update - May 12, 2010

Can't believe the change in the weather! What happened to our lovely spring days ? There are some new plants in Lian's garden that will probably have to be re-planted when she gets back here next week - we had a big frost Sunday night. The asparagus farms in the area lost most of their crop - will have to wait for new growth before they can harvest again.

[Lian, missing her mother's garden on her brother's farm near Woodstock asked if she could take advantage of the expanse of our back yard and put her own vegetable garden in here in Chatham since there was no space around their condo in Kitchener for her to do so.]

Radiation finished without any problems - just tiring to be on the road every day. The appointment time is never the same, so you have to plan every day differently.

Monday, we saw my oncologist again, after getting a chest x-ray in the morning. She was happy to tell me that it showed no appreciable change - no growth of the tumour ("That's GOOD news") Other good news was that I had put back on 6.5 lbs. since April 27, when she saw me last. My next chemo starts May 17 -

two weekly doses and the third week off; after 6 doses, another CT scan. I will be able to get this in Chatham, another piece of good news. So it was a fairly positive visit and we were encouraged. I continue to follow the nutritional advice of the nutritional oncologist I met in Austin in December and it seems to be helping as well. I have lists of things (drinks, supplements, etc.) to take every day and it keeps me hopping to remember them all.

On Friday, we were very pleasantly surprised to find that the whole Texas crew had come to Chatham, not just Steve. It was great to have the kids in the house again for a while, although the cold weather was a surprise for them and cut down on the amount of time to play outside. Pete and Jocelyn arrived as planned, so from Saturday morning until Sunday afternoon the whole crew was here. Pete left on his way to Brazil again; plans to be there for another two weeks, I think.

Based on my oncologist's comments in April, both weddings are being moved to June. The Kitchener one involves getting new dates for the same venues but the Seattle one will be moved to Michigan or something like that - total uprooting of all plans. Pete's travel to Brazil does not help this situation, as well as the time difference between Brazil and Seattle - 4 hours. Jocelyn is still working as a Gr. 7 English teacher, so there is marking and report cards to be taken care of as well. I appreciate so much that they are willing to do this but I feel so bad that all these great plans are going out the window.

Thanks again for the wonderful cards and words of encouragement that keep appearing in my mailbox - there is usually at least one every day. They are so good at lifting my spirits when I am having a 'down day' or they are just comforting, knowing that someone is thinking of me and praying for me. I appreciate them so much.

May God bless you today.

Post a Comment On: <u>Helen's Journal</u>
Jocelyn said... *Helen*

Thank you for posting on your blog; it helps to feel closer than we are out here in Seattle and down in Brazil.

Please don't feel bad about the wedding plans at all, we are coming up with a beautiful new wedding in Michigan. By tomorrow I should actually have some details nailed down, I will keep you posted!

You are in our thoughts many times every day. It was great to see you last weekend and we can't wait to get back out very soon.

Lots of Hugs

Jocelyn

<u>Tuesday, May 18, 2010</u>

<u>Update - May 18, 2010</u>

Good morning, one and all - had my first chemo in Chatham yesterday and am happy to tell you that it all went very well, if slowly. It was supposed to be a 15 min. dose, which actually took 6 min., once we got to that part. However, since it was my first time in that unit, there was a lot of introductory stuff that had to be done.

I was informed of all the side effects possible for this type of chemo and cautioned about a variety of things. I met my new supervising doctor and a new community health nurse. I came home with lots of new paper to read and a 'fever card' to use if I have to go to Emerg. with a fever over 38.5, which will help me 'jump the queue'.

I noticed on the orders for my chemo that my weight was wrong - off by about 10 kg. - and when I pointed that out, it lead to a check with my oncologist in Windsor and a new order, dispensing the chemo all over again - had to wait for that, too. You always get a saline flush of the veins before you get the chemo - takes 10 - 15 min., depending on how fast it's running, and a little rinse-out when you are done - just a minute or two.

All in all, we were there from 8:30 - 11:00 but they tell me it won't be so long next week. It's the usual start-up stuff. I felt fine all day yesterday and slept well last night; up at 7:00 as usual and have had breakfast and am doing my laundry as I write. So - pretty good, I'd say. I just hope and PRAY that the cancer responds to this chemo and that it has some effect on it, unlike the other two earlier this year.

I am really thankful for the peace of mind that I experience the majority of the time. Many of you are praying for that for me, and I thank you. It has been a lot scarier since February, when I found out that the first chemo wasn't working and I have had to make a much stronger effort to say "God is in charge and has my best interests at heart; He knows what He is doing." I am still doing everything I can to keep my body strong and to fight this thing but I am also very aware that whatever happens with the medications, etc. will be under His control. "Thou wilt keep him in perfect peace, whose mind is stayed on thee, because he trusteth in thee. Trust ye I the Lord for ever; for in the Lord Jehovah is everlasting strength." Isaiah 26:3,4. So that's what I try to do and am able to, most of the time.

More rain here again last night - we are pretty well soaked. It will be nice to get some warm, sunny days again.

Wedding plans are coming along - the one being moved from Seattle to Detroit will be much simplified from the original but will still be nice. Planning is taking place in Seattle, Brazil and Chicago, thanks to Skype. The Kitchener one is also experiencing some changes but will be more like the original plans. Steve is looking for a portable condenser for me that is strong enough; I won't need so many pressurized tanks when I am out of the house.

Thanks again for your prayers. May you too experience the peace of God today by trusting in His care for you.

Helen's pressurized cylinders of oxygen were becoming a burden to her. While she breathed much better with them, and we were thankful to the Canadian Government for paying for them, they were a nuisance. Many times we overestimated the useful time on one cylinder. There seemed to be slight variations in how full new tanks were, and often one that we counted on for three hours would run out after 2 ½ hours. Some times we made trips home from church or restaurants or other events, on empty; Helen trying to relax and breathe normally even though her oxygen had run out. I talked to the respiratory people to see if they could come up with a portable unit. They brought one for us to try, but my definition of portable and their definition of portable were two completely different ideas.

The unit weighed about 40 pounds, was the size of an upright vacuum cleaner, was noisier than our neighbour's combine and had inadequate battery life. We returned it within one week.

To Steve, desirous to do "something" in his mother's fight with cancer, this was a golden opportunity. It was a problem that needed solving and he was excited to get on with the challenge. He ultimately found a portable unit in Texas, that weighed about 10 pounds, was the size of a large lunchbox, came on a small cart like a pull-behind suitcase that could be detached and placed in an overhead compartment of an airplane, ran on 120 volt power in the house, 12 volt power in the car, and had a total battery life of 9 hours with two batteries on board, and a third backup battery with its own power supply that recharged it in half the time that it took for a battery to run down. Best of all, as part of his research, Steve had picked a unit that was FAA approved for any airline. On the Delta website it was at the top of the list of approved units that could be used on a plane. A non-stop flight to Austin from Detroit was under three hours. With nine hours of battery life it was a piece of cake. Helen could be airborne again! He brought it with him to the wedding in Detroit. When we crossed back into Canada after the wedding, we had a doctor's prescription showing that this was necessary to sustain Helen's life, and were processed through the border with no comment.

Friday, May 28, 2010

Update - May 28, 2010

Good morning - lovely day promised here in southern Ontario - hope you are looking at a similar one wherever you are.

My second chemo took place on Tuesday of this week - went much better than the first time. We were there 8:30 - 9:50 and everything went smoothly. I had a good talk with the super-

vising doctor who reassured me that my heart rate (over 100) is still within normal range, and I am not going to 'blow up' some day. I have been having a lot of trouble with coughing, too, and he advised me to double up on my GERD medication to help with that. Apparently I have a hiatal hernia but the surgical repair for that is not possible for me now. We went shopping afterwards and out for lunch, so it was a nice day.

Wednesday, we were in Windsor at the cancer centre again to see my oncologist. I was happy to be able to tell her that I have noticed a significant improvement in my breathing for about a week - I can go without my oxygen for 30 min. or so if I am just being quiet. She listened to my lungs and agreed - much better air return in the right lung! So, I guess the radiation is having a good effect, since it would be about 10 days before that I finished that. Possibly even the medication from Dallas - who knows? I am just enjoying it and the beneficial effects - I am more energetic, can eat better, can move better, etc. So interesting to see just how totally your body depends on its oxygen supply - you think it's the food you eat, and up to a point it is, but without oxygen, nothing works.

I have developed a lump on the top of my head which is going to have a needle biopsy some time in the next two weeks. Lots of possibilities, most of which make me nervous, but at least it is on the outside of my head. Because I had so many lymph glands that were 'positive' at my surgery, the cancer can move anywhere in my body. Breast cancer can move to lungs, liver, bones and/or brain. It's the brain part that bothers me because I would like to stay 'myself' throughout this experience. My dad's prostate cancer traveled to his brain and he went blind the last few months of his life as well as some other issues. But he was still there most of the time, so I guess I won't try to scare myself too much with all of that. I am just hoping that I won't have to have a big shaved spot on my head right before the weddings!

Also, last Saturday Amy, Lian and I went dress shopping in LaSalle for dresses for the two weddings. I was able to find two dresses and a pair of shoes that will go with both of them in just over an hour - more oxygen = more energy ! I am very pleased with both of them - I don't want to look 'invalid-y' - just make my boys proud of their mom at their weddings. I think I will be able to do that. They have done so much to make sure that I could be part of their celebrations.

There are so many people who are kind to me - I love my flower beds in the summer but can't plant them so well this year. I went and bought the flowers for the big one right in front of the house and a group of friends from church came over and planted the whole bed in an hour ! It looks so good and when I sit on the front porch, one of my favourite places, it is lovely to look at. Lian is out there watering them daily. I am such a wuss these days that I can hardly haul the hose out far enough to do that. When I think of what I was doing this time last year, it can get pretty frustrating, but then I just have to be glad that I am still here.

My pastor can over to visit the other day and read me some of the Psalms of David, in which he prayed for deliverance from his enemies. It's so interesting how those words apply to how I feel - I find myself praying the words from Ps. 59 - "O my God: defend me from them that rise up against me!"

Thank you to those of you who continue to send me lovely cards with such encouraging messages - I appreciate each one. They come from people I wouldn't always expect and sometimes have messages about things that I have done that I don't remember (good things!) but that they do - you never know what other people are noticing. Sometimes I feel like my whole life has just been one big 'seeding' operation and now the 'crop' is being returned. It can be pretty encouraging.

"Be careful for nothing; but in every thing by prayer and supplication with thanksgiving let your requests be made known unto God. And the peace of God, which passeth all understanding, shall keep your hearts and minds through Christ Jesus." Philippians 4:6,7

May God's peace be with you today.

Wednesday, June 2, 2010

Good morning - I thought I'd better remind everyone that this is my week off from chemo; nothing happening with that now until next Monday. It's two weekly treatments and then a week off; that's considered one cycle. I will have at least 6 cycles, if it works. Next Tuesday, I have an appointment for an ultrasound-guided needle biopsy of the lump on my head. I am quite anxious about that but there's nothing to be done except wait. I've found that since I started this journey, every physical twinge sends me thinking about the cancer spreading - is it or not? Sometimes you just have to turn your mind away from that and choose not to think about it. That may be a kind of 'ostrich' maneuver but it saves on emotional wear and tear and useless output of energy.

I continue to feel better and to be able to do more. Last Saturday, another group of 'garden elves' came to work on my big flower bed in the middle of the front lawn. My oxygen hose wasn't long enough to get out there, so after fussing on the front porch for a while, I just took it off, hauled a picnic cooler out for a place to sit, and visited with them as they worked. I was able to go without oxygen for almost two hours, which felt good. Several days later, in the evening, I was able to get the garden hose out, water the flowers in the front bed and put it back. I got tangled up with my oxygen hose once or twice, but David didn't laugh at me and let me sort it out for myself. It feels so good to be able to do some of these things again. Made a fruit salad for dessert Monday night when we had company, got supper ready to cook last night - still in the game.

My sister is driving here from Ottawa today and we will have a couple of days together; she'll be back again for the weddings in a couple of weeks.

So - that's about all the news for now - I'll bring you up to date again next week after I've had the biopsy and stuff.

God bless -

Saturday, June 12, 2010

Update - June 12, 2010

It's a lovely, quiet Saturday morning here - I'm the only one up and the house is peaceful. I'm thinking about putting on the air conditioning before things heat up, since today is forecast to be the hottest and most humid one we've had so far this year. I have found that humidity can really affect my breathing ability.

Well, chemo went well this past Monday - nothing much to it. We had had a quiet weekend with my sister coming for a visit from Ottawa and I was ready to return to the chemo routine. I almost forget about it - have to remind myself the night before. We were a little longer this time - 8:45 - 10:30 or so - not bad at all. The chemo medication comes in a little syringe - about 2 tablespoons of fluid - and it is injected into the IV line that is already attached to my port. I continue to pray that the cancer will respond to it and that it will have the desired effects of slowing and/or stopping the growth of this cancer.

Tuesday, we went to Windsor for the 'ultrasound-guided needle biopsy' of the bump on my head. This did not go as expected. The ultrasound did not show as clear a picture as the radiologist M.D. wanted before doing the needle biopsy, so a CT scan of my head was arranged. Of course, this involved another hour or two of waiting, but at least it was in familiar surroundings. After the CT scan had been read, the radiologist came and told me that the biopsy was not necessary any more - "we can see well enough what's going on in there with the CT scan". This was delivered in the hall of the hospital as well as a message that my oncologist would clarify it with me. So - we were all upset - what could it mean? Spent a few hours in mental turmoil. But we went out for lunch, and while in the restaurant I was reminded by that quiet inner voice of the verse which says "God has not given us a spirit of fear..." and I was able to return to a place of mental peace. We have not heard anything further and I am operating on the philosophy that 'no news is good news' The longer it takes to hear something, the less serious it will be. So we are just going on with our lives and getting ready for these weddings!

The first one is a week from today. Later today I go to get my dresses and things will seem even more real and exciting, once they are hanging in the closet.

My breathing continues to improve - I have spent several nights sleeping without my oxygen and can be without it for several hours at a time during the day if I am not too active - like typing out my blog! I have had it off for over an hour this morning as I have been doing this and it feels very good not to have the cannula on my face all the time. I still have a lot of coughing at times but we had recorded the conversation with the radiologist when we talked about doing the radiation and he mentioned that my esophagus would be inflamed from the radiation and I would have a lot of coughing and difficulty swallowing as a result. I had forgotten that part in the excitement of having my breathing improve so much.

Well, I think that's it for today - hope your day goes well and that you are aware of God's presence and blessing with you as you go about your lives.

Tuesday, June 15, 2010

Update - June 15, 2010

Good morning - kind of overcast here today and rain is expected for tomorrow but all indications are that Saturday will be warm and sunny for the first wedding! For the Texas crowd a day in the 80's will be a welcome cooling off from the weeks of 95's that they have been experiencing.

Chemo yesterday went very well - done by 10:30 or so. I was able to walk both into and out of the chemo lab - no wheelchair, as I had been doing when I started in May. This would be a distance of several hundred feet and I see it as another little measure of my general improvement and returning strength. I am so thankful.

The actual dose of chemo is 6 ml. If it proves effective against the cancer, I may be on it for some time, but we'll see how that develops.

We also had a very encouraging talk with the supervising doctor in the chemo lab yesterday. I told him about my CT experience in Windsor and he felt the bump again - told me it didn't feel like cancer to him, just a 'bone growth' - osteo.....something. He also told us that if the cancer seems to be 'retreating', as mine seems to be from the radiation at least, that it will not likely spread to other sites, like brain, liver, etc. That was excellent news to us and I was especially cheered since I have found it difficult not to assume that every new twinge or pain is an indication of the cancer spreading somewhere else. There are now always two voices in my head debating whether or not it is spreading - a sore elbow could be bone cancer...or just a pinched nerve. I think it is because the original cancer kind of sneaks up on you that you are never sure that it's not going to jump on you again somewhere else. You tell yourself not to be so negative but the other little voice says. "Yes, but...". Anyhow - this will help with all of that mental wondering and I was very glad to hear it.

Today is the last quiet day before the wedding schedule takes over - manicures, laundry, hair appointments, packing (trying not to take my entire wardrobe), ordering enough oxygen tanks, etc. It's going to be a lot of fun ! I am feeling really well and am so thankful that I will be able to participate in these celebrations with enthusiasm.

May God be with you today in whatever you are doing. Thank you again for your prayers and loving concern. I am happy to tell you that I am feeling so much better.

Tuesday, June 29, 2010

Wedding Report June 2010

The summary statement is: We couldn't have asked for more beautiful, enjoyable wedding days than the ones we were able to enjoy in the last 10 days. They seemed as if they had always been planned to happen when and where they did!

Wedding # 1 - Pete and Jocelyn

We left for Detroit on Thursday, June 17, in order to celebrate our own 43rd anniversary that night before all the other festivities and had a lovely dinner at a restaurant just a half-block from the hotel. Friday was a quiet day - we had breakfast with Jocelyn's parents, Jack and Martha Gruber, and David finally got to meet them. Later, I was able to help Martha make up the bouquets for the wedding, out of lovely calla lilies. Martha had been extremely busy, making various things for the wedding, including four boxwood-covered pillars that supported the letters L-O-V-E, which were to be background for the wedding. There were Welcome bags containing home-made cookies as well as other goodies for each guest, ribbon streamers to wave as part of the wedding, heart fans, etc. all in the wedding colours of white, black and apple green. Other family started to arrive during the day and by that evening we had a large dinner party going in the restaurant at the hotel - 20 adults at least and several children. It was a pleasure for us to start meeting Jocelyn's family, especially her 93-year-old grandmother, Fidelis, as bright as you could wish to be at that age.

Saturday was quite a day! The weather was perfect - sunny and hot. We started with breakfast at 8:00, then a rehearsal outside on the lawn about 9:30. Various objects were called into service to stand for the real thing, much like a pick-up hockey game and we went through our paces for later in the day. Pete and Jocelyn looked great and were so happy to finally be there and practicing for the 'main event'. After the rehearsal, there was a surprise lingerie shower for Jocelyn in her parents' suite - ended with a fabulous 'movie' set of long, black sheer wrap, bordered with black marabou feathers, black marabou-covered mules and a short black lace gown. Quite the ensemble ! I had my rest until 1:00 and then David and I went down for some lunch to keep us going - and who was on the elevator but his sister and brother and their spouses, who had just driven over from Chatham for the wedding! So - we all went for lunch and had a good visit. Shortly after 2:00 I realized that I still had to get dressed, so we dashed back to our room and got ourselves 'rigged out'. I was looking forward so much to wearing this fabulous dress that I had found and it just looked great. David wore his tux, as were all the other men in the wedding party. We made it to the lobby for 2:40 or so and were just in time to walk out to the wedding site on the lawn. It had been transformed - white folding chairs, the boxwood pillars and letters as a backdrop to the event, a white runner between the rows of chairs, flowers, etc. - looked fabulous; behind it all was the river, sparkling blue in the sunshine and all the boating activity of a summer Saturday afternoon. Steve had brought me a new oxygen converter, which meant that I didn't have to use the big, heavy tanks that I had been using when I was outside and this was a huge improvement for me. It is a small 'box' on wheels and can run on a battery for 5 - 6 hours at time.

The wedding started on time - we were escorted in by Pete and then the bridesmaid, matron of honour, flower children (Lily's green tutu dress arrived from the seamstress in Utah at 12:20 that afternoon), ring bearer (burier, according to Clay) and then the bride herself, wearing a gorgeous 'mermaid' style dress - strapless and fitted to just above her knees but then flared out into a fabulous, swishy 'tail' of several yards of fabric. Pete and groomsmen were all in black tuxes with black vests, except for Pete's which was white. Jocelyn was sporting black shoes, to keep with the colour scheme too, but we didn't see much of then because of the big skirt. Everything went well for the ceremony and it was done in a lovely and heartfelt way. It was obvious to all that the two of them meant every word they said to each other and their vows were blessed by tears.

Pictures were done on the spot - there was a large old brick building at the edge of the hotel lawn and that was the backdrop. So, people just scattered on the lawn and enjoyed the cocktail bar and hors d'oeuvres which were being passed around until they were called for their turn in the 'picture gallery'. Clay and Jackson, ring bearer and flower bearer, amused them-

selves in the reflections from the hotel windows, trying their hats at various angles and the rest of us amused ourselves watching them. The only really bad thing that happened at the wedding happened to the photographer, Kip - someone stole his equipment suitcase just before the ceremony started. It was sitting on the bar table and apparently someone just walked up and took off with it. He had switched cameras and was able to continue taking pictures - most of us didn't realize that it had happened until that evening. His equipment is all insured; what he wants back are the pictures in the cameras - many of which they were able to re-stage Sunday afternoon.

By 5:00 it was pretty hot outside, so we went inside to the reception and air conditioning. It continued to be a most enjoyable evening and I was pleased that I was able to stay for the whole meal as well as the speeches and some of the early dancing. I even got to dance a bit with my husband and with Pete, the groom. I am enjoying my returning health so much and one of the best reasons is that I can do some of the 'normal' things again. I was able to stay until 9:30 or so and felt very good about that. The party went much later but I didn't miss anything important.

Sunday morning saw a big family brunch at 10:30, which we all enjoyed. The two families really got along well together and that was one of the nicest parts of the whole event. It was a case of putting faces and personalities to names that had been heard and getting a sense of what the 'other family' would be like for each marrying child. We both were pleased and felt that they would be well looked after. At the end of the day, after everyone else had left, David and I had supper with Martha and Jack and Pete and Jocelyn. We went to an Italian restaurant right in the RenCen (Renaissance Center) in downtown Detroit, which also gave us a good view of the RiverFest going on that weekend. It was a lovely ending to a wonderful weekend.

Monday, after breakfast together with the same people, we left and came home through Windsor, where I had a chest x-ray at the hospital. We were able to visit with David's brother, sister and spouses as well as my sister for the next few days as well as Steve and Kristen and crew. David had his last Board meeting of the school year on Tuesday night - a marathon which saw him returning home at midnight. I'm not sure that I ever really unpacked!

Wedding # 2 - Mike and Lian

Thursday saw the exodus begin to Kitchener-Waterloo, although I guess Amy actually left Wednesday and others didn't leave until Friday. We got up there in time to go out for dinner that night with Amy and Mike and Lian at a most interesting Brazilian Grill House restau-

rant. Besides a salad bar, you are offered tastes of 8 different kinds of meat, all brought to the table on swords. Once you have tasted them all, you can choose more of the ones that you like. Nothing topped dessert though - a whole pineapple, also on a sword, roasted over the grill like the meat, seasoned with cinnamon and brown sugar. We were pleased to help finish off the one they brought to our table.

Friday was a quiet day for most of us until the rehearsal at 4:00. The ceremony and the reception were also going to be in the same venue for this wedding and I must say, it makes it much simpler for all concerned. The venue was another of the industrial sites being reclaimed in downtown Kitchener - The Tannery - which is what it used to be. Lots of old brick, exposed venting and pipes, but very clean and charming - a lot like the condo that Mike bought several years ago! The caterers were busy setting up the tables and chairs when we got there, so we could see how it was going to be. Guests would be seated at their tables for the reception when they arrived, there would be several rows of chairs for the family during the ceremony with an aisle in the middle leading to a clear space in front of the head table where the ceremony itself would take place. Mike and Lian were going to be married by David's brother Dan, a minister from British Columbia, who had a one-time license to do this service in Ontario. So - rehearsal went smoothly and we retired to the rehearsal supper, being catered at Mike and Lian's condo building on the rooftop garden.

This turned into quite an event - the weather was excellent, the food was unique, and at the end of the evening, several hot-air balloons were seen, which the kids loved. For food, there was catered food from a northern Thai restaurant, sushi and sashimi from a Japanese restaurant, chicken wings, Lian's father's signature duck meat salad, special 'rosette'-style cookies, beef curry, mango salad and, of course, lots of sticky rice to fill in the gaps. We had all of our family there - aunts, uncles, siblings, spouses and children and most of Lian's family too, plus the wedding party of friends, so it was a large and happy group. Once again, both families enjoy being together and we had a pleasant evening.

Saturday was as busy but not as scheduled as the previous week. Lian had a hairdresser and two make-up artists at the condo and I had booked in to get my hair done, so my sister got me over there for 10:00 or so. The place looked like a flower shop - there was a florist there making 12 table centre pieces, the centre piece for the head table, bouquets for the brides-maids, boutonnieres for the groomsmen - I don't know how she got them all done but they looked fabulous. There was even time to get hot apple fritters from the St. Jacob's market when the trip was made to get Lian's bouquet. I knew I had to rest, so I had to leave about 12:00 to go back to the hotel.

We stopped on the way - it was now raining heavily - and bought some yogurt and other snack-type foods that I could use for a lunch as well as some nylons, because it was getting fairly cool and my dress was light. (A lovely ivory silk, with magenta, purple and greenish flowers, kind of water-coloured onto it.) I couldn't remember the last time that I bought nylons - has to have been years. But I got back in time and had a good rest and then started getting ready. We were both decked out and ready to go by 3:30 and headed over to The Tannery, just 5 -6 blocks away.

Fortunately, it had stopped raining by the time we were going there, so we got in without incident and went and sat down - turned out that the chairs were mostly for our side of the family because we didn't have a table - it would be brought in after the wedding. Things seemed well under control and everyone was pretty calm, even Mike. Guests were still arriving after 4:00 but eventually we got under way - probably about 4:15, which isn't too bad. We were escorted to our seats by Mike and then the rest of wedding party followed. Lian had made the dresses for the three bridesmaids and maid of honour, as well as one for the 'groomslady' with Mike. Colours were purple and ivory. Other groomsmen were in tuxes with a lovely gray tapestry vest. Clay and Warren [Lian's nephew] were in tiny tuxes, too and Lily, as flower girl, had a lovely ivory floor-length lace dress, so everyone was 'lookin good'! Finally, it was time for the bride - who had made her dress too - lovely ivory silk with appliquéd lace flower panels, strapless and fitted to about the knees and then flared out in the back to a big, poufy train - and dad Chat, looking so proud in his tux as well. (For those who wouldn't know, Lian's beloved mother, Khem, passed away in March 2009, after a short and unpleasant battle with pancreatic cancer.) The wedding proceeded smoothly except for one part, which Mike will continue to hear about. He didn't wait long enough when it came time for the first vow and responded with a heart-felt "I will" when Dan said, " Mike will you take this woman to be your lawful wedded wife..." it made everyone laugh and set the tone for an informal, comfortable mood for the rest of the wedding.

When it came time for the reception, one of the highlights was when Lian changed into her Thai wedding dress, She had bought the material in Thailand when they were there in November. It was a lovely ivory and gold silk, top and skirt and it was so nice to have this additional cultural element to the wedding. Mike changed into an ivory jacket and they looked wonderful together. We were able to get some pictures with them, which I am looking forward to seeing. Then they changed back again into their original wed-

ding garments when it was time for the toasts and other parts of the reception. I particularly enjoyed the toasts of the groomsmen, including one from Mike's former housemate, Brian, who could not attend. It's always interesting to hear remarks about one of your children from those who have lived with them and know them well. Granted, it was his wedding and they were going to be polite, but you can still get a pretty good idea. We were able to stay for part of the social time but left between the bride's bouquet toss and the groom's garter toss - apparently a good decision, from what I heard later! Although Clay was wearing the garter as a belt when I saw him the next day, so I don't know how that all happened.

Sunday morning, we met at the hotel dining room at 11:30 for a brunch together before everyone started to leave. My sister Carol had already left, as she was driving back to Ottawa via Kingston, but we had breakfast together before she went. We sat with David's sister, brother and spouses and had a nice time just being together. We never know when we will have the chance again - British Columbia and Minnesota are not next door to Ontario. Then it was time to break it up and everyone left to check out and leave. Once again, we were staying until Monday, but everyone else was leaving at some point Sunday.

I heard that Pete and Jocelyn were going to go over to Amy's to do a laundry, so I hitched a ride with them - David was going to catch up on his sleep. I wanted to have more time with them because I never know when I will see them again, either. It turned out very well in the long run, because Steve and Kristen arrived with their crew, Pete and Jocelyn decided to stay longer and we all went out for supper together - an unexpected bonus. About 7:00 p.m., Pete and Jocelyn headed for Detroit so that they could make their 6:15 a.m. flight to St. Lucia the next day and Steve and Kristen left for Niagara Falls, to have a few tourist days before they return to Chatham later this week. Amy will join them Monday. Mike and Lian are also in the Grimsby/ Vineland area for their honeymoon.

Finally, we loaded up all our stuff Monday morning - well, closer to Monday noon - drove over to Amy's for a short visit and picked up the two dogs and headed peacefully for home, happy to have been a part of two such wonderful events and full to the brim with family time and love. I was also so thankful that I was well enough to participate so much and to bring the blessing of my improving health to my children and husband and sister, who have been through so much with me this spring. God has been so good. Thank you all for all your prayers for all of us through this wonderful time.

Monday, July 12, 2010

<u>Update - July 12, 2010</u>

Good morning – hard to believe it's been this long since I updated the blog but things have been busy, as you will see.

We came home from the weddings two weeks ago today – arrived home about 3:30 in the afternoon from Kitchener. I went out for groceries about 5:00 p.m. and as I was arriving back home at 5:30, David saw me and decided to come and help. He stood up quickly, forgetting that he needs to be slower and to wait, because of his vertigo problems. He made it to the door of his den, realized that he was going to fall and turned to go back to his desk chair. He didn't make it – he passed out and fell, striking his face on the edge of his desk and falling with his head under it. I was in the house by then and rushed in to see what was happening. I could see that he was bleeding but not from where.

He was groggy and couldn't move himself, but in a few minutes he was able to roll over onto his back and out from under the desk. He had bruised his face and was bleeding around his left eye. I decided an ambulance was the only option and he agreed. He was taken to ER after being checked out and eventually had 6 stitches under his eye. However, he is on blood thinners and that caused tremendous bleeding; most of his face turned dark purple and his eyes were terribly swollen for a few days. He still has vestiges of the bruising two weeks later.

A neighbour saw the ambulance and came over to check it out. She took me to the ER and stayed with me, eventually bringing David home as well. It was quite shocking and very painful for him as well; he had a headache for several days and didn't wear his contacts because of his bloodshot eyes. Most of that seems to have passed now. I was very impressed with the ambulance crew – their kindness and their efficiency.

A week ago today, I had two doctor's appointments in Windsor. In the morning, I saw the radiologist, who confirmed that the treatment the first week of May had been very effective in improving my breathing and reducing the tumour that was restricting the airflow. I do not need to see him again unless my oncologist feels it is necessary. (This would be because there was another tumour in my lung that was possibly treatable by radiation.) In the afternoon, I saw my oncologist and the news from her was more mixed. She showed me my two chest x-rays from May and June and pointed out the improvements – less compression of my heart, more breathing room in my right lung – all very good news. This shows that the new chemo is having an effect and I will be staying on it indefinitely (as long as it is working, at this point.) I have a weekly treatment for two weeks and then the third week off. The bad news was that the lump on my head is a bone metastasis and that the cancer is spreading to bones as well as lungs. However, she was quite matter-of-fact about it and said, "This is what it is; this is what we are going to do." I am now on an additional medicine called Aredia which is not chemo but a bone-strengthener. It is also used for osteoarthritis. Tuesday, I went for my chemo in Chatham and wound up getting the Aredia right away. It didn't have any effect at the time, but I had a low fever that night and spent the next two days in bed, just wiped out. I didn't feel nauseated or anything – just had no energy and actually slept for part of Wednesday, quite unusual for me. I'm still coming around from it and do not feel anything like I felt at the weddings – but there are other contributing factors to that, I'm sure. I will have a treatment of Aredia every three weeks.

Amy was with us all week and Mike and Lian came down for part of the weekend but everyone went home last night and today it's just David and I.

I'm struggling with this bone cancer diagnosis; I was feeling so well at the time of the weddings that I thought I might get a break and be 'normal' for a while. Now I have to figure out what this means and what consequences I will have to deal with – not too positive the last couple of days, I must admit. However, I have been reminded by several family members that I am much better than I was in April and that I have just come through a fairly intense time of travel and emotion and I should give myself a break. So I am trying to do just that. I'm really not a good patient – I can cope with an illness as long as I don't feel bad!

I know that God is still in this with me and I continue to trust in His guidance – blindly, sometimes, like a little kid hanging onto a parent's hand or coat – but trusting in the knowledge, wisdom, purpose and love of the One who is leading. Thank you so much for your prayers – there are so many of you who are so kind to remember me.

Chapter Nine

The Final Months

Tuesday, July 27, 2010

Update - July 27, 2010

Good morning – two weeks since I last reported in but I have quite a bit of news to tell you.

Last week was quite busy – on Monday, (July 19) my chemo day, it was discovered that my hemoglobin was down to 81 (from the normal 120 or so) and I almost didn't get my chemo. (This happens when you are given chemo over a long period of time – it destroys fast-growing cells and the red blood cells in your bone marrow would be one of the ones 'under attack'. They said it was surprising that I hadn't already had a transfusion, due to the amount of chemo that I have had.) I was scheduled for a blood transfusion Wednesday morning – 2 units and 4+ hours to do this! Then Tuesday afternoon, I already had appointments in Windsor for a CT scan and bone scan. For the bone scan, you get a needle of radioactive dye that has to circulate through your body and you have to wait while it does that. I got the needle at 1:30 but had to wait for the scan until 4:15 – and then it took most of an hour. Lots of practice waiting ! The rest of the week was fairly quiet; a good thing, because it was still very hot and humid.

Amy came back Sunday to be with us for my chemo yesterday morning and also for the trip to Windsor to hear about the results from the scans. I was quite anxious – more than I realized – and afraid that I was going to hear that my bones looked like Swiss cheese. However, God is good and so was the news ! I have only the two metastases on my head – lumpy head – and the CT scan showed that my liver is still clear, so I am clean, clean, clean except for the cancer in my lungs. Such a relief !!! The doctor explained that the CT scan also showed progression of that cancer since April but that she didn't feel it was accurate – that I had dropped farther after the CT scan in April than we realized and was now on the upward swing but still not back to where I was in April. However, I feel extremely well and everything is working very well – breathing especially – so we are going with that. The blood transfusion has helped with my energy levels – no red blood cells, no oxygen, no energy – and my colour is better too – according to onlookers!

We celebrated this good news by going to a Red Lobster in Windsor and ordering lobster ! Haven't had one for years ! It was quite an exercise – they don't cut it open for you as some places do, so you have to wrestle it 'to the ground' all by yourself. But boy! Did it taste good!

We are contemplating actually going away on a weekend trip to see if we remember how to do it – haven't been too many places since all of this started. We did make it up to a park on the St. Clair River south of Sarnia, one of our favourite places, to have a little picnic a week ago Sunday and enjoyed that. For those of you who don't live in this area, that's the river between the USA and Canada, and between Lake Huron and Lake St. Clair. You can look across and watch road traffic in the USA on the other side and if you were a good swimmer you might be able to swim across. There's always a good chance of seeing a lake freighter, too – pretty impressive at close quarters.

So I am very happy to report this good news to you and to thank you once again for all your support and prayers, especially during the last few months when things looked pretty black. I think it's safe to say that I'll be here long past October now but each of us only has today and I am still practicing living in 'now'.

May God's presence be known to you today.

Wednesday, August 4, 2010

Update - Aug. 4, 2010

Good morning - not much to report this week. It's my 'week off' and I have nothing medical happening at all!

Last weekend, we made plans to drive to Dublin, Ohio, where David used to live and work. However, at the last minute, David's vertigo acted up and he felt unable to drive. I was all packed and primed to go somewhere, so we agreed that I would drive to Kitchener and spend the weekend with Amy. I enjoyed the drive and felt that I had taken another big step back towards a more normal life. (It's about 2 hours from here.) I also had time with Mike and Lian, who live in the same city.

This coming Friday evening, Pete and Jocelyn are having a reception in Seattle for their friends who could not make it to Detroit in June. Amy, Steve, Mike and Lian are all going to be there. I will be there in spirit, as David probably will also, but that's as close as I can make it. Even if I took the trip out there successfully, it's not starting until 7:00 PDT (a reasonable time, to be sure) but that is 10:00 p.m. EDT and I am usually done and horizontal long before that. So, I will wait to hear the stories.

That's pretty well all there is to say for now - just a regular week, normal life, trying to keep up with the house chores and figure out what to have for supper, the perpetual question. Hope you have a good week at whatever you are up to.

Post a Comment On: <u>Helen's Journal</u>

*Gail **said...***

Boy you never know what is going on with your neighbours. Glad to hear that you are still feeling pretty good through all of this. Hope you have a wonderful weekend with the family. I don't know how we all got to be 65 but it's something to celebrate.

Gail

<u>Thursday, August 19, 2010</u>

<u>Update - August 19, 2010</u>

Good morning ! It's been a while since I updated this blog, but things have been happening again, as you will hear.

Last week, I had a chemo treatment on Monday (Aug. 9) as well as my second dose of the bone strengthener, Aredia. I was expecting to have a few 'down days' after that, as I had had the first time, but fortunately, that didn't happen.

No reaction to anything ! Wednesday afternoon, I was at the hospital for a respiratory test to see if I need additional oxygen (would support funding for this.) It also went very well. However, on Wednesday David also began to notice that the cloudiness in his vision that he had been experiencing since July 28 was getting worse – big 'floaters' in his left (good) eye. When he woke up Thursday, he could hardly see out of the eye at all and was quite concerned, as the vision in his right eye is still not 100%. He called the optometrist for an appointment and we went in Friday morning.

When the optometrist looked at David's eye, he decided to call the surgeon in London who had treated the right eye and we were asked to come up there as soon as we could. Fortunately, Amy had come here Thursday, intending to just pick up her dog, which had stayed with us while she was in Seattle the previous weekend. So – off we went, Amy driving. The surgeon –

and several other people – had a good look in David's eye and decided that it wasn't immediately critical – but that we should return for the clinic at 8:30 Monday morning. This is at the Ivey Eye Institute, at St. Joseph's Hospital in north London, north of Oxford and Richmond, if you know the city. For us, it is a 90 min. drive, so that meant up and out by 7:00 a.m.

After another careful check Monday morning, the surgeon decided that there was a tear on the retina and that he would 'spot weld' around it with a laser, to keep additional eye fluid from leaking in behind it and tearing it more. (The cloudiness had been caused by blood from the retina tear.) So – laser treatment (which hurt) and instructions to return at 8:00 a.m. Wednesday, in case there had to be further surgery. Wednesday(yesterday)we got better news – the weld is holding but it needs more time to heal. No surgery needed – but come back next Tuesday (Aug. 24) for a check at

1:15 in case there needs to be surgery the next day. In between, on Tuesday, I had my second chemo treatment of this cycle, which went well, as usual.

So – no dull moments, still ! Amy was a real trouper – stayed with us and drove all the trips to London and then took herself off home Wednesday afternoon. We had been to London and back, including breakfast out, by noon that day ! She will return Friday, with Steve. This coming weekend is my 65th birthday – not sure how that happened – but we are looking forward to a family dinner together Saturday night. Pete is winging through from Seattle via Detroit on his way to Brazil again and will be here about 24 hours and Mike and Lian will come down Friday night or Saturday morning, once Mike gets over his jet lag from his trip to China this week. I can't believe how the world of business just says casually to people – 'Oh – you have to be in *** next week. Have you bought your ticket?"

The amount of money spent on business airfare must be staggering.

Keep on praying, please !!

I will conclude by saying that I feel great and one could say almost healthy – just a little short of breath. I have to travel with my portable oxygen converter but it lets me go almost anywhere by myself. I also have to expect to be very tired by the end of the day and not get discouraged – a night's rest and I am 'topped up' again. So things are really going very, very well for me. I appreciate all your prayers and concern. God has been so good and I am so thankful for each day.

Thursday, August 26, 2010

Update - August 26, 2010

Good morning ! All is well on our front! We returned to the Ivey Institute this past Tuesday for David's eye check-up, prepared for the news that he might have to have surgery the next day. However, the report was great – eye was stable and healing and nothing else was necessary at that time. So we happily returned home and enjoyed a Wednesday free of appointments.

I had no treatments this week, either, so it has been a quiet time for both of us.

This followed a lovely birthday weekend for me – by Saturday, all four kids were home and we had a great time together. Steve took over the kitchen and fed people as they arrived but we went out to our favourite restaurant for supper. By Sunday they had to start leaving again but we had a good time together while it lasted. Pete was not on his way to Brazil as I had thought – he made a 'boomerang trip' from Seattle to be here and Steve flew up from Texas. Time together is the gift that I think I value the most anymore and I appreciated so much the effort that all of them made to be here.

Plans are in the works for Amy and I to fly to Texas for Steve's birthday in September. We'll be there for a week and I'm very pleased to think that I can do this and also that I will be able to be in Texas again. So – I really am feeling better!

Thank you again for your prayers and loving support. Hardly a day goes by without someone sending a card or some other thoughtful gift. I appreciate it all so much. May you be aware of God's presence with you today as you go about your life.

Update - September 20, 2010

Good morning! I have not updated this blog for almost a month, so there is a lot to tell you.

The last week of August and the first week of September were pretty quiet – just the usual stuff. I had chemo on schedule; David had another trip to London for an eye check-up that went well. We enjoyed going to a pig roast one weekend and having lunch with another couple as well. I had a couple of solo lunch and dinner dates – an enjoyable time and I was feeling pretty good.

However, the Saturday night of Labour Day weekend, I had a lot of pain in my side during the night and I asked David to take me to Emerg. Sunday morning. We were there the whole morning – another CT scan and chest x-ray – and lots of waiting. However, I do have to say that they took me right in – didn't even 'touch down' in the waiting room. The verdict was that I had a lot of fluid around my right lung but in light of my plans to fly to Texas later that week, doing a fluid drain at that time was not a good idea. So, home I went with a prescription for pain pills.

Two days later, (Tuesday) I had a regular appointment in Windsor with my oncologist. She had some concerns from the CT scan I had had in July and did not realize that I had had another one Sunday morning. She was unable to call that up (the hospitals are linked wirelessly) and did not want to make a decision about the fluid either until she had seen the most recent x-ray and scan. She is concerned that the cancer might have invaded my liver - NOT news I wanted to hear. However, not much I can do about it. We left it that I would have a regular appointment again Oct. 6.

Wednesday, Amy arrived after her own doctor's appointment, which went very well. We packed and got ourselves ready for an early departure the next day. I was concerned to leave David for that long because of his dizzy spells and when Amy arrived and saw how he was, she called back to Kitchener and asked if Lian could come to Chatham for longer than the weekend planned. Lian agreed; she'd arrive by supper Thursday and stay until Wed. morning. So, I felt much better about that – Mike would be down for the weekend, too.

Thursday morning we set off in high spirits to drive to Detroit to catch the plane. It is a direct flight to Austin of 2.5 hours – very doable on an oxygen concentrator. We had expected a lot of checking for my machine, but nobody was interested. I am able to be a 'wheelchair person' and that gets me a lot of other advantages getting through the airport to the gate. We had a good flight, Steve was waiting in the luggage area and it was 93F ! Yeah, Texas !

We had a wonderful week there. Amy had rented a little house through HomeAway.com that was only a few blocks from Steve and Kristen's house, right in the neighbourhood that we knew. We just loved it ! Very well appointed and attractive. We had lots of meals out, lots of visits with Kristen's mom, lots of good times and helped Steve celebrate his birthday. I saw Clay's school and classroom (got the full tour!), went to his violin lesson, watched Emmy working on learning to crawl, and Lily just enjoying life. (Lily is 2 and likes to be barefoot so that she has better traction.) The last day, Steve and Kristen treated Amy and I to a morning at Lake Austin Spa, which we all enjoyed. Amy and I had facials and manicures and Steve and Kristen had pedicures – Steve wound up with 'shiny toes'. It was a great day.

We returned to Detroit Thursday to a rainstorm and 60F weather – I wanted to get right back on the plane and go back to Texas. While we had been in Texas, there had been a call from my oncologist's office saying that I had the fluid drain scheduled for Friday, Sept. 17. I was a little anxious (How big will that needle be, anyhow?) but it turned out to be quite easy. The radiologist removed 1.2 L of fluid; an 'after' x-ray showed that there was still more, so I might have to do it again. If so, it will be no problem.

Mike and Lian returned this past weekend and did their usual magic around the house. All my big 'jungle' of tropical plants are safely back in the house for winter, back grass is cut, lovely meals prepared and eaten, groceries bought

– all the things that I used to be able to do so effortlessly. We appreciate the help and love of our children so much. I truly don't know what we would have done this year without that.

Today we have a doctor's appointment for David to see if we can get some answers to these dizzy spells – I am hoping and praying for help for him with that.

So – things are going well, although the possibility of liver involvement is scary. I should find out more about that in October. Sometimes I feel like there is a monster lurking in my body, ready to pounce when I least expect it and that is very unnerving. However, those are also the moments when I have to make a conscious decision to trust in God's ongoing care for me and turn away from that fear. Regardless of the outcome, I know that I live 'under the bubble' of His care; nothing happens to me that He does not know about or is not able to help me with.

I just have to keep looking at Him and not the monster.

May God keep you today, wherever you are and whatever you are doing.

P.S. to Update for Sept. 20, 2010

David had a very positive visit this afternoon with the internist and has several tests scheduled, which we hope will go a long way towards finding the answers to these blackouts and collapsing episodes. He will see the doctor again Oct. 13 and we hope to have some ideas then.

Update - October 7, 2010

Good morning, one and all ! Good news to report !

I had my monthly visit yesterday with my oncologist in Windsor and she gave me good news. There is no evidence of progression of the cancer, there is nothing going on in my liver (there was some question of that in Sep-

tember and I was braced yesterday to be told it had spread there) and she is going to make arrangements for me to have a permanent drain inserted to get the fluid off my lung to help my breathing. She said I might even be able to get off the oxygen, which would be amazing. (Nurses would come to the house to take the fluid off on some schedule – it wouldn't be leaking all the time or anything like that.) So David and I were a happy pair when we left the building ! To top if off, we were only there 1.5 hours ! We are very thankful for my continued good health, for the medicines that are keeping it that way and for God's mercy, which underlies the whole thing.

Last week, David had a bone marrow aspiration and tomorrow he will have a CT scan of his head, looking for any blockages that might be causing the dizzy spells and black-outs. There has already been mention made of anemia – news to us. He goes back to the doctor Oct. 13 and we are hoping for answers to the mystery.

We set off on a 'weekend away' last Thursday, Sept. 30. Our Texas son, Steve was in Waterloo on business, so we all had supper together that night – Amy, Mike and Lian were all there as well. It was great to see them – had breakfast in St. Jacob's the next morning, too. Then David and I left to drive to Wiarton on the Bruce Peninsula, where he had a school board regional meeting. It felt like we were driving right to the North Pole, but that just shows you that we are soft southerners. We had a good time – found a nice little café on the main street there which served excellent food (Green Door Café). Then Sunday, we drove 351 km. down Highway 21, along the eastern shore of Lake Huron. It was a lovely drive – the lake is so blue and the leaves are all turning. It was sort of a test case, to see if I could travel that far at a time, and it worked out very well.

We have so much to be thankful for this weekend ! May God bring to your minds and hearts all the blessings that you have experienced as well. Thank you again for your prayers.

In Wiarton, on the shores of Georgian Bay (part of Lake Huron) we had a lovely time. I had booked the hotel room for two nights, the Friday night before our Saturday regional school board meeting, and also the Saturday night. We had a conventional room the Friday night so as not to abuse the taxpayers' money which was paying my education related costs, but Saturday night on our own money I had reserved their best suite. It include a "Franklin Stove" a cast iron stove with the ability to open both front doors to form a fireplace. It also had a Jacuzzi nestled into one corner of the huge bedroom. I told Helen that I would pass on the hot tub, but she wanted a few minutes to soak. She undressed and attempted to get into the tub. I was distressed to see her unclothed and to see all of the weight she had lost. By this time she had lost about 50 pounds, and she looked very frail. It took her about 5 minutes to actually get into the tub, sitting first on the edge of the tub, and then slowly swinging one leg over the edge into the water. After resting for a few minutes she slowly swung the second leg over, and then "skootched" herself around until she was sitting on the end of the tub, and then allowed herself to slip into the water.

When the time came to get out, she was unable to do so by herself. I gently lifted her out of the tub, and stood her up. She was too weak to dry herself, so I took a towel, carefully dried her off, wrapped her in the towel and hugged her, choking back tears at what this insidious disease had done to her beautiful body.

We said nothing about the episode the next day, and enjoyed a delightful trip south. Just south of Owen Sound she directed me onto a concession road and pointed out to me a farm house owned by the family of one of her "Winston Posse" to which the group was scheduled to go for a few days at the end of October. She was delighted to realize that we had proven that she could make the trip that distance up and back, and she was looking forward excitedly to that trip. We stopped in the little town of Bayfield, near Goderich for lunch, and discovered a delightful restaurant with great food. We had a wonderful few days together, never realizing that this was to be our last road trip together.

Canadian Thanksgiving, the second Monday in October, was a blessed time. Helen was never happier than when she had all of her children gathered around her dining room table and could cook a sumptuous meal for them. Helen began preparations on Saturday. Amy came down on the Friday to do the heavy lifting for us, and to help with preparations. Helen was taking particular enjoyment from having Lian in her kitchen, eager to learn exactly how Helen made her pie crusts, and how she made her pumpkin and apple pies in particular, so that Lian could go back home and prepare these things for her husband Mike. Helen left the pies until she knew Lian would be here. Because of our limited number of attendees, Helen chose to forego a turkey this year and purchased a chicken capon instead. However, all of the "fixin's" including stuffing, mashed potatoes, squash, cranberry sauce, both pumpkin and apple pie, and of course her signature squash soup were all in waiting for Thanksgiving Monday to arrive.

We had a wonderful time around the table on Monday as most families do. It was a significant day, because the Sunday, the day before, was originally to have been Mike and Lian's wedding day, and the April prognosis suggested that Helen would no longer be alive by then. We opened a bottle of champagne to celebrate that fact, and Helen raised her glass and said "So there, cancer. I'm still here" and we drank to that toast with exuberance. We had no way of knowing that we were experiencing our last family dinner, that in six days Helen would shed her weary body and take on a perfect body in Glory.

God does not let us see the future for a reason. It could be terrifying. I am thankful that He does not. We had a marvelous weekend together, Helen and I had a great week together and last day together, enjoying our time to the fullest because we had each day, and a commitment to take each day as a gift and relish it. Ignorance of the future is a gift from God. Seize it with confidence knowing that He knows the future, and He cares for us.

Chapter Ten

Helen's Graduation

My father's parents, brother and several sisters were members of the Salvation Army. We as a family attended the Salvation Army until I was about five years old. Many of my aunts' and uncles' funerals were conducted by the Salvation Army. There seems to be a standard bulletin that is used for the order of service for Army funerals, on the cover of which is boldly printed "Promoted to Glory."

As I mentioned in the introduction to this book, Helen had decided that her passing was going to be her "graduation," complete with graduation music.

October 16th, dawned like any other day, with beautiful sunshine; a perfect fall day. We went to a Tim Horton's for breakfast, and then generally putted around for the day, doing some grocery shopping and other errands. We went for a drive out to the shore of Lake Erie. There is a conservation wetland there which is a nesting area for a pair of swans. Helen loved the migrations of swans and geese and we hoped that we might see some resting on their long flight. About 5:00 PM I went and got take-out Chinese food, a favourite of both Helen and I. We ate in the living room while we watched a movie. I cannot remember anything about the movie, except that it was very funny, no one was beat up or shot, and there was no foul language. In retrospect it must have been a 100 year old rerun. About 8:00 PM Helen decided that she was going to go up and soak in the tub and read for a while. From the living room I heard her fill the tub, and then heard the motor of the Jacuzzi start. It ran for about 45 minutes and then I heard the tub empty. About 9:00 PM she called down the stairs that she was going to bed and for me not to stay up all night. About 10:00 PM I headed upstairs to go to bed myself. As I reached the top of the stairs, I heard her voice calling "David, I need you." I ran into her bathroom and found her coughing up blood. Those words were to be the last words she said to me. I told her that I was going to take her to the ER, and since she was in her nightgown to come and sit with me on the bed and tell me what clothes she wanted on to make the trip. She came and sat beside me, but did not turn her head to look at me nor did she answer me. I began to rub the middle of her back where coughing often caused muscle pain, and became conscious of her pushing against my hand. Confused I let my hand and arm swing back, and watched her slowly lie back on her bed. When I saw her face, her eyes were staring into emptiness, her mouth was open and her jaw clenched, there was a slight yellow, waxy appearance to her skin, and I knew she was gone. She had graduated!

I called 911.

Our next door neighbour saw the lights of all of the emergency vehicles in the driveway and immediately came over. When I told him what happened, he went back to get his wife. There is a bureaucracy to a person dying, and Don and Penny sat with me while the Paramedics attempted to revive Helen, as the police interviewed me with three different officers asking questions in slightly different ways, as they had to fulfill their responsibility to rule out domestic violence as the cause of her death. We waited while a Paramedic consulted with our family doctor who certified the nature and time of death by telephone based on the Paramedic's input. We waited until the coroner was reached by telephone and approved the removal of Helen's body, and then waited while the funeral home people attended to that. In the process our pastor, a police chaplain, who had been contacted by the police came to the house with his wife. In all, Pastor Gord and his wife Pat, and my neighbours Don and Penny sat with me until 3:30 in the morning. After prayer by Pastor Gord, as they all rose to leave, Don offered to sleep on my couch so that I would not be alone in the house. I declined because I still had telephone calls to make. My youngest son Michael was airborne on a 14 hour flight from Toronto to Tel Aviv, Israel for a business trip. It would be three hours after his mother's death before he was back on the ground and anyone could reach him. I called Helen' sister Carol and broke the news to her. I talked to all of my children except Amy, who I could not reach on her cell phone. Often when she retires for the night, she turns it off and has no landline at her house. I finally went to bed about 6:00 AM.

Helen had been fearful of death, and passed away about 20 seconds after realizing she had a problem, seemingly painlessly, peacefully, sitting on her own bed, in her own bedroom, in her own house, with her husband's arm around her. It doesn't get much better than that.

At 7:00 AM Amy and Lian walked through the front door. Steve arrived early in the afternoon. Peter and Jocelyn took a "red-eye" from Seattle and were in the house early the following morning. Mike was stuck in Tel Aviv waiting until Wednesday when he could get a return flight. Kristen would arrive later in the week with the three children in tow. For a variety of reasons I decided to put Helen's funeral off for a week, to give us all time to assemble, grieve privately and reflect on the wonderful person that had been sister, mother and wife.

Monday, October 18, 2010

This is Helen's husband David. This will be the final update to this two year description of a woman of faith, a fighter, a woman who loved her family fiercely, and a woman to whom the love of an incredibly close knit family was returned.

Helen passed peacefully into the presence of our Lord and Maker Saturday evening, October 16, at about 10:00 PM She had had a very "normal" day, a long soak in the evening in our Jacuzzi, and then went to bed about 9:00 PM. At a few minutes to 10:00 as I made my way upstairs, she called out to me. She was in her bathroom coughing, and was spitting up blood. Since she was only in her nightgown, I asked her to sit with me on the bed and tell me how she wanted to be dressed for the trip to the ER - just a housecoat and slippers, or what. She walked out of the bathroom, turned and sat down along side of me. Since coughing often gave her a muscle pain in the middle of her back, I began to rub her back as I talked.

I immediately became conscious of her pushing against my hand, and she slowly lay down on her bed. As soon as I saw her face I knew she was gone, but performed CPR to the best of my ability after calling 911, while waiting for the Paramedics. When they arrived in about 10 minutes, all of their tests only certified what I already knew. She was already "arrayed in a white robe" slipping into the alto section of the choirs of Heaven, radiant in the face of her Saviour. She and I both had strong apprehensions about "the end" based on experiences of friends and loved ones. That her passing was virtually instantaneous, and painless, was a gift from God.

Also a gift from God were the months we shared together since her diagnosis in July of 2008. We had time to make all arrangements for both of our funerals, and put all of our legal, financial and insurance affairs in order, together. We had 28 months to laugh and love together, to make some trips including Texas several times to see our grandchildren (and their parents !), we were able to welcome into our family a third grandchild, to see our two younger sons married to wonderful young women, and time just to sit and hold hands on the couch. God was so gracious to us.

As we made this journey together, we discovered that there are a multitude of angels in our midst, disguised in the garb of doctors, nurses, and volunteers in the Windsor Regional Cancer Centre (WRCC), and the Chatham-Kent Health Alliance (CKHA). I am afraid to name people for fear of missing someone, but I would like to thank foremost, Dr. Caroline Hamm of the WRCC. Dr. Hamm is a fighter, and together with Helen was not prepared to ever back down in the face of this monster, cancer. She was always confident, professional, and exuded a sense of determination, from which Helen and I drew great strength. I would also like to thank Dr. Khalid Hirmiz (WRCC) for his courage and skill with radiation, and his tenacity in destroying or shrinking tumours in Helen's lungs, enabling her to breathe easier. To Krista Naccarato (WRCC) who guided us, literally and figuratively, in the early days of treatment, through a clinical trial, we always were where we had to be, when, thanks to Krista.

In Chatham, I want to thank Dr. David Sullivan, for his bonhomie as he made his daily visits to the chemo suite, for his gentle but practical care, ensuring that treatments were tolerable, and that Helen had no pain, and could rest at night.

In both Windsor and Chatham, the nurses in the actual chemo suites were comforting and caring combined with their professionalism. They had many "little touches" like Karen in Chatham, who every day brought in a box of her mother's homemade cookies. I would like to thank Chatham nurses Cheryl Jarescni, Karen Kennedy, Jackie Opavsky, Dianne Jackson, and Colleen Janssens. I am sorry that I do not know the names of the Windsor nurses, as I spent most of my time there in the waiting room. However, Helen was quite outspoken about their care, compassion and skill. Not to be outdone were the volunteers in both locations, like Ben in Windsor, who always kept the waiting rooms flowing with Tim Horton's coffee and cookies, and who spent hours talking with me and encouraging me when not busy with his tasks.

When Helen was part of a clinical trial in Dallas TX, she received the same compassionate and attentive care from Dr. John Neumanitis and Cindi Bedell at the Mary Crowley Cancer Clinic, as she receive from all other medical professionals. Thanks, y'all!

I also want to thank our caring and helping neighbours, Chuck & Gail Scott, Don & Penney

McLellan, and Robert & Beth Stewart. Chuck or Gail would magically show up at the front door with a delicious meal every couple of weeks, while Don and his son James must have real vision problems, because since this spring, when either of them was cutting their front lawn, they would somehow wander off course, and cut our 18,000 square foot lawn. Robert owns what looks like the biggest John Deere in the county, and when snow would clog our 180 foot driveway, he would be there without us asking, to make sure we had access to the road. He has cleared our drive in this fashion faithfully since about 1978. Angels hidden amongst us don't just play harps.

Helen was a woman of tenacious faith, a loving partner, a dedicated mother, a wonderful musician, and a committed and outgoing teacher. She touched lives through her personality, her music, her "grand piano smile," her infectious laugh, and her genuine interest in the well being of other people. She treasured her children, including our "chosen daughters," chosen for us by our sons. She reveled in her grandchildren, delighted to see them growing and maturing, whether in person or through frequent "Skype" sessions.

She was a soul mate, companion, lover, and friend to me for over 45 years, 43 of which as my bride. I was incredibly proud of her and her accomplishments. She was more than my "better half," she was my strength, my joy, my "pull me back down to earth dose of realism" person, my comfort in sickness, pain and times of sadness, but also my high-kickin' partner in times of great joy. I will miss her deeply. It was my delightful privilege to be her husband and friend for 43+ years!

She had so many circles of friends from whom she drew support, and I cannot name them all. However I must mention her "Winston Posse" a group of teachers and retired teachers all of whom taught at Winston Churchill Public School in Chatham at one point in their careers. I think this group has been together for 12 or 13 years, publishing a yearly itinerary, which included something for each month ranging from dinners at fine restaurants to female retail therapy at a mall in Michigan at least one a year. This spring, when it was obvious that Helen could not plant the beautiful flower gardens that she loved, "garden elves" materialized from this group and friends from our church, and voila! Beautiful gardens as usual.

Finally, I need to thank all of the prayer warriors who upheld her daily. I lost track of the number of the various prayer chains in a multitude of churches who blanketed her in prayer, but I know on any given day there were probably over 1000 people who remembered her. We received great support from our church family here in Chatham, and I want to thank Pastor Gord, his wife Pat and all of the multitude of people at Gregory Drive Alliance Church. I also want to thank a dedicated group of believers known as "The Encouragers Class" at Dublin Baptist Church in Dublin Ohio. It was our joy to worship at that church during the time I lived and worked in Dublin, and even though it has been almost 9 years since I left Ohio to retire back in my home town, that group has stayed in touch, sent cards, letters and e-mails constantly. DBC pastor Daryl Gabbard has remained in touch with us and on several occasions has called to encourage us and have prayer with us on the telephone.

For Helen's sister Carol, my brother Dan and his wife Leona, and my sister Barbara and her husband Cliff, I thank you for the years of sharing, trips together, laughter and bad jokes. In the melding of multiple families, I think we were the cream of the crop.

Helen's funeral will be on Saturday, October 23, 2010, at the Gregory Drive Alliance Church in

Chatham, Ontario, at 11:00 in the morning. Friends and family are invited to come and share memories on Friday, October 22, 2010, at 3:00 to 5:00 in the afternoon, and 7:00 to 9:00 in the evening at the McKinlay Funeral Home at 459 St. Clair Street in Chatham.

Should you wish to make a tribute to Helen, I would ask that instead of flowers, that will wither and die in a few days, that you make a donation to the Foundation of the Windsor Regional Cancer Centre, where your tribute will live on and will help people like Dr. Hamm to research and treat this monstrous disease to the benefit of other patients and future generations. Thank you.

I also would like to thank you faithful readers who followed her blog. As we checked the statistics on the blog this morning, since its inception, it has not been unusual to have over 1000 "hits" every month, and numerous comments with each posting.

In closing, I would like to put here a "prayer of faith" that Helen wrote in this middle of her fight with this disease. I think she may have included this in a post earlier, but it bears repeating.

A Prayer of Faith

O God !
Have mercy, I pray !
Deliver me from the onslaught of these fears -
These dark imaginings,
These dreadful possibilities that are only that -
Possibilities - NOT facts.
They roll over me like the waves of the sea,
And fill me with despair.
Help me to realize that the voice that whispers
them in my mind
Is neither mine - nor yours.
Help me instead to turn my thoughts to You -
To remember Your precious promises
Given so often and so clearly in Your Word -
To comfort and sustain,

To defend and protect,
To fight for those who put their trust in You.
Help me to go over them, Lord,
The ones You have given me,
Word by word,
Promise by promise,
Step by faltering step,
Until I reach Your peace -
Until I am enfolded by the Comforter -
Until I am safe in the light of Your love -
And I can truly speak the prayer
That never fails -
"Thy will be done."

Thank you, O Lord, my God,
For Your sustaining love and grace.
Amen.

Post a Comment On: <u>Helen's Journal</u>
*Gail **said**...*

Dave, what a wonderful tribute to Helen. She will be missed by so many people. Gail

<u>Sunday, October 24, 2010</u>

This is David again. In the previous posting to Helen's blog, I said it would be the last entry. It turns out I grossly underestimated the outpouring of love by so many people and I need to make at least one more entry.

I was overwhelmed by the people who visited at the funeral home Friday and the number who attended her funeral on Saturday. We had planned visitation Friday for the time periods of 3:00 PM to 5:00 PM and then from 7:00 PM to 9:00 PM. Visitation started as planned at 3:00, and continued until 10 minutes to 7:00 when I was able to grab a slice of pizza that the funeral home had purchased. I was back at Helen's side at 7:00 and the last visitors reached the coffin at

10:30. Many people stood in line for over three hours. Approximately 600 people came to the funeral home to honour Helen and to support me and my family.

One of the most touching parts of the day was the young people who came with tears in their eyes, to tell me of the influence Helen had on them as their teacher. About 70 former students visited Friday. The other thing that I had a hard time comprehending was the distance people drove to be with us. Excluding family members, there were friends from Ohio, Michigan, Quebec, and some a considerable distance from Chatham, from Wingham, Wawa, Toronto, Ottawa, Waterloo and Windsor. One couple spent all day Friday driving from Georgetown Kentucky to be with us.

Helen's funeral was lovely, and touched people in attendance. I was so proud of our children – our "original four" as they spoke words of tribute to their mother, and our chosen daugh-

ters as they supported their husbands. Helen made a phenomenal investment in her children, putting aside her teaching career for 18 years to raise them. Financial people talk about return on investment, and Saturday I was reaping the return on Helen's investment. Our children have cared for us for the past many years, and stood strong with me by their mother as she battled this disease.

At the funeral, we listened to a couple of songs recorded a few years back – one a duet of Helen and I singing "It is well with my soul," one of a solo by Helen and one of a 1965 college chorale in which both Helen and I sang. In attendance at her funeral were 6 or 7 members of that same choir. As I listened to Helen's beautiful contralto voice sing "why should I feel discouraged, why should the shadows come?... when Jesus is my portion, my constant friend is He ... His eye is on the sparrow and I know He watches me" I felt strangely at peace as I thought that voice will never be silenced, and now sounds even better than Helen did in person.

I want to thank Pastor Gord Reynolds for his care in the past week, and for his role in celebrating Helen's "graduation." I thank my brother Dan, for reading on my behalf, the eulogy I had written, and for his words of comfort at the graveside committal service. Thank you Marjorie Hall for your loving hands on the piano, and thank you to the ladies of Gregory Drive Alliance Church for the reception you provided after the funeral.

To Rob McKinlay, and his staff at McKinlay Funeral Home, thank you for your courteous and professional help provided in such a compassionate manner. I entrusted to you the care for my mother and my father in years past, and now Helen.

To my family members including my extended family linked through my chosen daughters, who travelled here from British Columbia, Minnesota, Florida, Texas and Woodstock, thank you for making the circle complete. To my many cousins who stood with me, and who I know will be there for me in the days and weeks ahead, thank you.

And to all of you who came, to the funeral home or the church, or both to pay tribute to Helen, thank you.

To the residents of Chatham-Kent, drivers of the 100+ vehicles that pulled off to the side of the road and stopped out of respect as we made the procession from Chatham to Union Cemetery in Pardoville, thank you. Our family and friends from the USA asked me if there was an unusual traffic law in Canada that required vehicles to stop. As I explained that this was not a requirement, but a respectful, local tradition, I was proud to be a resident of Chatham-Kent.

One final touch was a large flock of geese, which flew over as we reached the cemetery.

Helen's Journey

Helen loved watching the Canada geese, and Tundra swans fly over on their migratory journeys. Often when she would hear their honking, she would run out of the house for a better look, and never failed to be excited by their passage. As we reached the cemetery, Pastor Gord pointed out the fact that the geese looked like an air force fly over.

There are many benedictions in the Bible, but Helen's favourite was Jude 24-25.

"Now unto Him that is able to keep you from falling, and to present you faultless before the presence of His glory with exceeding joy, to the only wise God our Saviour, be glory and majesty, dominion and power, both now and ever. Amen."

Helen was laid to rest in Union Cemetery in Pardoville Ontario on the north shore of Lake Erie. Adjacent to the cemetery is a small country church, built for the community by a Mr. Pardo for whom the community is named. The church sat vacant for some time, and then in 1967 the Gregory Drive Alliance Church in Chatham decided to re-open it and make it a daughter church. My father was asked if he would be the pastor, and for 15 years he and my mother ministered there together during his last years working for Chrysler and in his early retirement years. My parents are laid to rest just a few feet from Helen's grave.

As my brother spoke the words of a committal service, the silence was broken only by the occasional call of a gull. When Danny finished speaking each person present took a red rose from a container. In her coffin, Helen was wearing one of my rose corsages, and I stepped up to her coffin, reflected on what a gift I was given and the privilege to be her husband, and then said "Good night, sweetheart" and placed my rose on her casket. Each person in turn placed their rose on top of the coffin and blanketed with 30 roses, we committed her temporal body to its rest, knowing that in her spiritual body she was rejoicing in the presence of her Lord.

She was an exceptional woman. The visitation at the funeral home was estimated by funeral home staff to be the largest visitation ever witnessed since the business was established. She was a caring teacher, a dedicated mother and a loving wife. I am a richer man for having been allowed to share her life.

"See you in the morning, sweetheart!"

Helen's Journey

Christmas 2009

Helen's Journey

David and Helen

Everpresent Oxygen Leash

Helen's Journey

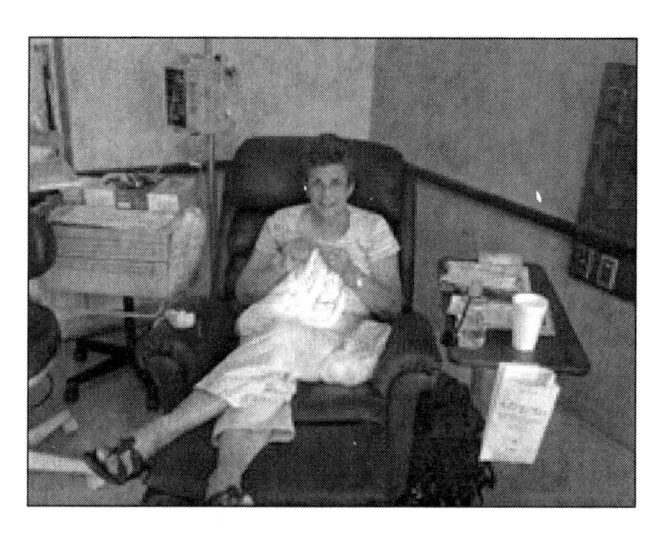

First Chemo Knitting

Helen's Journey

Grandma Time

Last Mothers Day

Helen's Journey

Last Texas Trip

Helen's Journey

The Second Wedding

Helen's Journey

Treasured Grandchild

Helen's Journey

Who Has More Hair